Schrifttanz

SCHRIFTTANZ

A VIEW OF GERMAN DANCE IN THE WEIMAR REPUBLIC

Valerie Preston-Dunlop
and Susanne Lahusen

DANCE BOOKS
Cecil Court, London

First published in 1990 by Dance Books Ltd., 9 Cecil Court, London WC2N 4EZ, in association with the Laban Centre for Movement and Dance, London

© 1990 Valerie Preston-Dunlop

Distributed in the United States of America by Princeton Book Co., PO Box 57, Pennington, NJ 08534

British Library Cataloguing in Publication Data available

ISBN 1 85273 016 1

Production and design in association with Book Production Consultants, 47 Norfolk Street, Cambridge

Typeset by Cambridge Photosetting Services, Cambridge
Printed in Great Britain by Biddles Ltd, Surrey

Contents

List of Illustrations

Foreword

It was a wonderful experience for me when, one day, I was surprised by the news that the work I had been involved in 60 years before, which had since fallen into oblivion, had suddenly come back to life. The product of youthful enthusiasm is now unearthed and exposed to criticism, asking whether it can be cited as material for the documentation of a decisive period in the history of dance.

My involvement with dance began in my early youth. Since I had the good fortune to have been born in Dresden at a time when progressive elements in all the arts provoked much attention and excitement, my adolescent curiosity was strongly encouraged. What became the decisive factor after I had finished grammar school was my time at the Dalcroze Institute, in Hellerau near Dresden, where I participated in courses. There, beneath the columns and the magical light of the dance temple of Tessenow, an inspired way of life was born, shared by teachers and students alike. Rhythmic exercise gave me the opportunity to apply and further the musical knowledge which I had earlier acquired. Visual awareness complemented musicality. I developed an interest in all kinds of artistically inspired movement. In this atmosphere my international outlook and tolerant nature were strengthened, which made it possible for me to make many friendships in the Wigman School at that time. I was a frequent visitor there and gained many insights into its work.

After leaving Dresden, I systematically made contact with as many 'movement artists' as I could find. The great variety of personalities – and in particular the friendships with Laban, Jooss, Schlemmer, Nijinska, Chladek, Gert and Jodjana – created for me one fascinating experience after another. Every meeting strengthened my impression that we needed a forum. This would give creative artists the opportunity to make contact, to present new work and new ideas, to exchange information and to discuss common problems. The most obvious solution was a journal.

The first attempt, in 1922, was a failure. Emil Hertzka, director of Universal Edition in Vienna, to whom I presented my plan, rejected it. I think my *Wandervogel* attire irritated him and made him suspicious (later he was to become my role model). Approaches made to other publishers proved to be equally unsuccessful. I looked for another way to bring dancers together. The idea of organising a dancers' congress emerged. Niedecken-Gebhard, the director of the municipal theatre in Münster – a great dance enthusiast who had engaged Kurt Jooss to establish a modern dance group and had given me the job of producer – was delighted by the idea. Towards the end of 1926, we all went to Magdeburg, where a theatre exhibition for the next year was in preparation. We succeeded in making the First Dancers' Congress a part of this exhibition. One of the successful repercussions of this, combined with my becoming an employee of Universal Edition, was that I was able with the help of Dr H. Heinsheimer to get Hertzka's permission for the publication of both scores in Laban's notation and the journal *Schrifttanz*.

Alfred Schlee
VIENNA, JUNE 1989

Preface

The publication of this book has grown from the ongoing research project, the Laban Collection, sponsored by the Laban Centre and the Gulbenkian Foundation. During a collecting trip for the project in Vienna in 1985, an almost complete set of *Schrifttanz* was found in the Theatre Collection of the City Museum.

Alfred Schlee, the first editor, was still a director of Universal Edition, and was prepared to share his memories of the dance explosion of the 1920s, including *Schrifttanz*. Back in London, dance scholars at the Laban Centre worked on the texts and it became clear that *Schrifttanz* included material which gave an insight into many facets of the German dance of that time.

The publication of *Schrifttanz* has to be seen in the context of the whole of the Laban Collection programme. The primary aim is to collect evidence of the beginnings of twentieth century modern dance in Europe, with an emphasis on Laban, in the form of a working collection for scholars. Audio and video tapes, written material, and artefacts have all been collected, catalogued and protected on microform, to date some 16,000 items. The second aim is to work on the materials in order to identify and fill the gaps in knowledge of the period. It is well known that the Nazification of Germany and the exile of artists wrought havoc on European modern dance. The bombing of the major German cities during the war destroyed much archival evidence. Many personal collections and theatre and newspaper archives were burnt. No comprehensive history of German dance at that time exists nor indeed has a comprehensive biography of Laban, the leading reformer, been written.

The collecting work undertaken by Dr Preston-Dunlop has entailed many months of searching in the relevant libraries and archives all over Europe, and of interviewing individuals still living, in an effort to gather together both the personal data and the professional work of the dance artists of the period. The Collection is incomplete and still growing, but has been an invaluable resource of primary material particularly enabling us to contextualise *Schrifttanz*.

The Laban Collection work has also a practical component. A programme of Laban's Kammertanz dances made in Hamburg between 1922 and 1928 was mounted by Laban Centre dancers in July 1987. The purpose of re-creating such material is to give dancers today a direct experience of the 'New German Dance', an awareness which the written word alone can never give.

The Collection has given rise to several articles and research projects focussing on the era, and the present volume is the first book using this resource to be completed.

V.P.-D.   S.L.

Acknowledgements

We would like to thank Dr Marion North and the Research and Faculty Development Committee of the Laban Centre for Movement and Dance for financial assistance; Charlotte Purkis, Laban Centre research assistant, and John Dunlop, Laban Collection archivist, for discussion on translations; Ilse Loesch in East Berlin, Gertrud Snell in Hanover, Aurel Milloss in Rome, and Alfred Schlee and Fritz Klingenbeck in Vienna for sharing their experiences of this period with us; David Leonard for encouragement; The Mary Wigman Archive and the Goethe Institute Library for special assistance with historical references; and John Dunlop for clerical assistance. Without all these helpers, this book would not have come into being.

V.P.-D.   S.L.

Introduction

The journal *Schrifttanz* started its four-year life in 1928. It was edited by Alfred Schlee, a young member of the staff at the well-known music publishers, Universal Edition of Vienna, on behalf of the German Society for Written Dance. It was an act of faith on his part prompted by Rudolf Laban's convincing presentation of his new notation system for movement and dance at the Second Dancers' Congress in Essen in the same year.

The original intention of the journal was to provide a forum for the introduction and discussion of written dance, that is of dance written down in its own symbol system. The first preface by Dr Ewald Moll, chairman of the new Society for Written Dance, states it as such. But rapidly a much broader vision of the meaning and the role of *Schrifttanz* emerged, that of written dance encompassing all aspects of dance writing including history, criticism and the theory of dance practice. Four editions a year were envisaged.

The journal settled into a regular format. From the third edition on, the front cover presented a drawing by an artist well known as a designer for dance. The work of Schlemmer, Larionow, de Rego Monteiras, Georg Kirsta, Hiler, Heinrich Heckroth and Picasso provided the readers with the visual impression of an up-to-date and artistically oriented journal. Between five and eight articles formed the main text, which was followed by notices from the Society for Written Dance. Addresses of notation correspondents for 22 German cities and also for Switzerland, France, the USA, Czechoslovakia, Yugoslavia and Latvia were listed in the first edition.

By 1929 the notices were of more general interest – mainly announcements of forthcoming dance performances, tours and lectures by leading personalities. They were wide-ranging in scope and reflected the variety of dance activity of the time. Excerpts from the January 1929 edition's notices are given as an example. They quoted tours by Ida Rubenstein's group to European capitals, by Harald Kreutzberg and Yvonne Georgi to the USA and by Dussia Bereska's group to northern Italy. Premières by Mary Wigman, the Paris debut of Vera Skoronel and Oskar Schlemmer's performances in Berlin were listed. A forthcoming music and dance event in Paris was announced; so too was a public meeting in Berlin led by Laban and Wigman to explore plans for a State College for Dance. New works for opera ballet groups and the appointment of ballet masters were included. New members of the Society for Written Dance were announced and, inserted as an enclosure, was a short piece of notated dance, an excerpt from *Green Clowns* (Laban/ Bereska), with verbal explanation.

The insertion of notated material was repeated in several editions. It consisted of reading exercises for teachers or short scores showing the wide use envisaged for the notation. Social dances, actors' moves and jazz dance were there to be read.

Advertisements completed each edition. Amongst them the journal *Anbruch* for modern music, *Singchor und Tanz* for theatre singers and dancers, and Joseph Lewitan's new magazine *Der Tanz* were regularly promoted. So too were Universal Edition's sheet music publications. *Music for Dancers, New Ballet Music, Dance Pieces, Danceable Piano Music* and *Orchestral Work for Dancers* are titles which appeared alongside announcements of Summer Schools and of the first dance notation textbook.

In the main *Schrifttanz* attracted original writing. The material for the first edition was all from Laban's circle – Fritz Böhme the dance historian, Hans Brandenburg the art critic and writer, Lizzie Maudrik the ballet mistress and Wagner-Régeny the composer – but writers and artists from a wider context, such as Oskar Schlemmer and Bronislava Nijinska appeared later. A lively exchange of views was the result, and this gave the journal a stimulating content of genuine discourse entered into by people intent on promoting a serious approach to dance.

Schrifttanz was short-lived. It was too specialised a publication to survive. Even today scholarly dance journals have only a small circulation, but in 1928, when dance scholarship was only beginning, it could not attract the general dance reader. As the economic depression worsened it became evident that *Schrifttanz* was not financially viable. In 1932 *Der Tanz* took it over. A much more popular magazine covering all genres of dance, *Der Tanz* weathered the economic storm, but within two years the Nazification of literature had begun and by 1937 *Der Tanz* was forcibly closed down.

Translations of the complete set of *Schrifttanz* would not have provided a readable book. Some of the articles were so strongly context-bound that they required more than editorial introductions to make them understandable. Some were parochial in their scope while a few others had content now better expressed elsewhere. The deciding factors in the method of selection were that the articles should promote an awareness of the issues in dance of the period, and that the balance of topics in the journal as a whole should be maintained.

The articles are grouped not chronologically but according to content. In this way we were able to give editorial material a clear purpose, namely to introduce a discussion area and give it relevant historical context. In order to place *Schrifttanz* in its literary context, information on the other magazines in which dance was discussed are listed in an appendix. Wherever possible, brief biographical notes are given on contributors.

The translating has been difficult. The German language style is dated and a suitable English version of some words and phrases has proved elusive. Where this is obtrusive the German is given with the English in parentheses.

V.P.-D. S.L.

CHAPTER ONE

The Search for New Directions

Editorial I

Germany, at the turn of the century, had no strong indigenous classical tradition. As in most of western Europe, ballet had an extremely low status, and the role of the male dancer was virtually non-existent; ballet no longer was considered a form of art, it merely served to provide light entertainment during opera performances. The only ballet achieving popularity during this period was Hassreiter's *Puppenfee (Fairy Doll)*, created in Vienna in 1888. It was also in Vienna that Grete Wiesenthal and her sisters, having started their career with the State Opera, rebelled against the rigidity of the classical style and created their own freer version of the Viennese waltz.

In Germany, the seeds of the new dance were sown by Rudolf von Laban in Munich, where he lived and worked during the winter months from 1910 to the spring of 1914. He began to free dance from its dependence on both music and prescribed steps, confronting the dance medium itself and its innate possibilities.

In the summer months he transferred his work to Monte Verità at Ascona. There he joined a group of writers, anarchists, anthroposophists, naturists, artists and philosophers; all were searching for an alternative way of life in which the human being could function harmonically, both within and despite the industrial and bureaucratic society of the twentieth century. The Asconans, through communal living, aspired to the great Romantic ideal of being in close touch with the physicality of nature and natural forces. It was inevitable that dance should play an emphatic role, because of its crucial theme of the ultimate in physicality, the body. Already during the Wilhelmine period, *Körperkultur* (best translated as 'culture of the body') had emerged as a means of self-fulfilment. It expressed the yearning to escape the frustrating effects of city living and industrialisation. The *Wandervögel* youth movement epitomised the groups which, variously, aimed at the harmony of body, mind and soul through physical activity in the open air, heightened by a strongly shared concern for ethical values.

Asconan concerns were rooted in similar ideals, but the spectrum of the Asconans' activities was much broader. Their concept of wholeness was epitomised by Laban's School of Art, where he taught *Tanz, Ton, Wort und Plastik* (dance, sound, word and the plastic arts), alongside efforts to achieve self-sufficiency by growing food, building a shelter and making clothing. He experimented by crossing traditional boundaries between art media, between performance and experience, between theatre and nature, between ritual and dance as art, and between the spiritual and the physical. His *Sang an die Sonne* (*Song to the Sun*), performed in 1917 on the mountainside, was an all-embracing creative event, which became a symbol for the spirit of Monte Verità.

In contrast to these Romantic idealists were the Dadaists in Zurich, who also rejected bourgeois values, nationalism and war. But the Dadaists' approach was iconoclastic and even nihilistic. They questioned the aesthetic and the function of the work of art and the role of the artist, through the 'events' of their Cabaret Voltaire which completely overturned all conventions of theatrical performance. Several poems, recited simultaneously, from back to front, in several languages, incompletely, with an upturned waste-paper basket over the head, serves as an example of their activities.

The Dadaists' nihilistic approach provided the second point of departure from which the European modern dance developed in 1919. One of the Laban dancers who participated in both Dada and Asconan events was Mary Wigman. As the star pupil in Laban's wartime school in Zurich, she was the centre of critical attention in the Swiss press. Her independent career as a dancer, teacher and choreographer began immediately after the war. Her passionate and vibrant dynamic and her prolific output in the early 1920s reflected the pioneering spirit in the arts of the Weimar Republic. Simultaneously, Laban commenced his multifaceted career in Germany by creating major experimental theatre works, establishing dance as celebration through his movement choirs and continuing his search for dance theory and literacy. The New German Dance was established, primarily through the endeavours of these two artists. It was variously called *Moderner Tanz, Absoluter Tanz, Freier Tanz, Tanzkunst* and *Bewegungskunst;* but the name which has remained is *Ausdruckstanz*, translated variously as 'expressionistic dance' or 'expressive dance', which associates the whole movement with Expressionism in the visual arts.

However, by the late 1920s, when the German modern dance had reached a period of unprecedented artistic activity, Expressionism in painting had already become largely a movement of the past.

German Expressionism first manifested itself consciously with the foundation of 'Die Brücke' (The Bridge) in 1905. Influenced by 'Les Fauves' (The Beasts) and Edvard Munch, 'Die Brücke' was led by Erich Heckel, Ludwig Kirchner and Karl Schmidt-Rotluff, and it included at various times Max

2

Pechstein, Emil Nolde and Otto Müller. The group's ideal was one of collective endeavour combined with individual creativity. Intensity of emotion expressed through vibrant colours became its hallmark, and the distortion and fragmentation of reality became its method. At the end of 1911, when 'Die Brücke' in Dresden began to dissolve, another group came into being in Munich, calling itself 'Der blaue Reiter' (The Blue Rider). Its most important representatives were Wassily Kandinsky and Franz Marc. Kandinsky sought to take Expressionism into a sphere even further removed from representational art; he sought to free painting from the object altogether and thus heralded the new term 'Abstract Expressionism'. His aim was to create a harmony of colours analogous to the harmony of notes in music.

Thus, by 1912 painting had already begun to turn away from its original Expressionist concern with raw emotion. An increasing number of painters began to reject the search for meaning as a starting point for artistic creation. Instead they sought to establish the primacy of form. Form was considered to be meaningful in itself, as Kandinsky argued in his famous essay 'Concerning the Spiritual in Art'.

In order to appreciate the issues discussed in Alfred Schlee's article, one needs to understand the various strands both in dance and in painting which are presumed to be covered by the term 'Expressionism'. A number of distinct developmental lines in dance are evident in the work done in the 1920s and the early 1930s.

On the one hand, in Oskar Schlemmer's work at the Bauhaus, precedence was given to the exploration of space, the geometry of the body and clarity of movement, while rapturous Dionysian performances were evident in the self-expressive work of the vast number of amateur dancers and some of the *Einzeltänzer*. These were solo dancers who, especially in the pre- and immediate post-war period, toured Germany with work in their own style, some with little or no training.

Wigman's work uniquely combined rapture and form, while Laban's work at his Choreographisches Institut continued the exploration of the medium, developing it into the discipline of choreology. Nevertheless, the prevailing image, however simplistic, of the New German Dance was, and still is, that of insufficiently disciplined self-expression.

Schlee raises further interesting points in his statement: 'The new dance has not been able to devise a new technique which might have replaced that of ballet.' The first issue is whether the German modern dance ever set out to produce a technique of its own, and the second is whether it ever intended to replace ballet. Laban regarded his work as within the tradition of dance. His book *Choreographie* is based on ballet, his space harmony forms are presented as a development of the ballet's geometric structure. Ballet's set vocabulary of steps, however, was not a starting point for him; but it was for his pupil Kurt Jooss, who expanded and adapted the steps to provide the Jooss/Leeder technique. Mary Wigman developed her own methods of training the body which, emphatically, were not based on ballet. None of these three set out to replace the classical technique. In fact, at his Choreographisches Institut, Laban taught the means by which the established vocabulary might be expanded, altered and fragmented, through the use of choreological principles of movement. Schlee's remarks were well justified, for there were many dancers who were totally opposed to the restrictions and conventions of not only ballet technique but of technique as a concept, a movement given impetus by Isadora Duncan. She saw her function primarily as inspirational rather than instructive. As in the United States, techniques associated with individual artists – such as Günther, Chladek, Bodenwieser, Wigman and Jooss – emerged, but these were not fully established until the 1930s.

The article by Galpern raises the issue of the confrontation of the ballet world with the more radical representatives of the German dance of the period. Galpern illustrates the frustration of the ballet dancer. His writing shows the narrow band of aesthetics of the body, of line, of dynamics, of musicality acceptable to the traditional ballet advocate, and the difficulty of looking at and appreciating the elements of the new which cross those boundaries. The new dance had other criteria and inevitably other forms, which were difficult for the ballet community to look upon with anything other than a derogatory eye. Using the criteria for dynamics of dance as an example, the new dance proposed to use, in both works and class, the whole range of *Spannung/Entspannung* (tension and relaxation), from hypertension to collapse to swing to vibration, simply because this whole range of dynamics was available. While individual artists from the ballet, such as Nijinsky, had already pushed the art far beyond its traditional limits, none of these innovative elements had reached the ballet classroom – except in Bronislava Nijinska's School of Movement, which is discussed later.

Berthe Trümpy's reply to Galpern raises a number of unpleasant issues, but it has to be understood in context. The idea that particular styles and types of dance are inextricably linked to one culture, and are inappropriate in another, is not new. This assumption is exemplified by the suspicion afforded to the elements of black culture which came to Europe through jazz and popular social dances. Despite the great cultural diversity of the Weimar Republic, there was a strong and steadily growing nationalism present in the German people. Germany had, after all, only been a unified country since 1870, and this unity had been greatly shaken by the events at the end of World War I – in particular by the provisions of the Treaty of Versailles, which were seen by the German people as punitive. The need to re-establish self-respect and national pride was evident in the arts, as elsewhere. Trümpy

4

voices a view held by many of her contemporaries, both on Germanness itself and on the need for purity in the New German Dance. Only those dancers who were able to see the New German Dance from a wider viewpoint as part of a developing art, alongside ballet, were able to find ways of moving forward; thus avoiding the abusive confrontation evident in Trümpy's writing, which led nowhere artistically and indeed culminated in its downfall.

The two quotations chosen by Trümpy express extreme points of view which nevertheless contain a tendency which we can all recognise. Trümpy is taking a stand, typical of many who refused to acknowledge the existence of the middle ground: 'Ballet as such is not an art, it has nothing to do with art. All attempts to create a synthesis of classical and modern dance are therefore bound to fail.' History does not support her view. Starting with Kurt Jooss and Aurel von Milloss, there are many successful examples of just such a synthesis.

Valeska Gert regarded herself as neither a ballet dancer nor a modern dancer. A strong individualist, she experimented early with most of the *avant-garde* movements of her time, participating in the mixed-media evenings of the Berlin Dadaists, Kokoshka's Expressionist play *Hiob* and Ernst Toller's *Die Wandlung* (all in 1919). She included acting in theatre and film, cabaret performances and mime in a career which was highly successful through her unfailing instinct for caricature and social comment.

Not unlike that of the painters George Grosz and Otto Dix, the style and content of her art often went beyond the limits of bourgeois acceptability into the realms of the grotesque, contributing to a phenomenon typical of the Berlin of the 1920s. A concern for the spiritual which she mentions was common to many artists of the period, but in her case it took an interestingly different form. Whereas Mary Wigman concentrated on the dark side of things spiritual, eschewing realism and searching for abstracted means to express the essence of her subjects, Valeska Gert did not shy away from realism, even if it meant dealing with the uglier aspects of human behaviour.

Her emphasis on the importance of the performer's allographic use of the movement material, according to the mood and emotion of the moment, her awareness of the audience as an active participant in the dance event and the effect of the theatre space and ambience on the whole, show the depth of her artistry in a new genre.

During the early and mid-20s, when Schlemmer's 'Bauhaus Dances' were performed, audiences did not yet fully recognise the importance of his work. His article in *Schrifttanz* in 1931 is proof of his disillusionment. He clearly emphasised the importance of spatial elements, which he saw as the unifying principle for all Bauhaus artists, in his choreographic work. His work was often misunderstood – critics described his dances as 'mechanical' or even 'dehumanised'; yet from Schlemmer's writing it becomes clear that man was always at the centre of his work. He regarded technique and clarity of form as essential for liberating the artist from chaos and confusion.

Fritz Böhme's article shows clearly that by the late 1920s there was a need to find distinctions between the different dance forms which were less simplistic than the one between ballet and modern dance. Fritz Böhme's terms *Podiumtanz* and *Theatertanz* are no longer used and therefore an immediate parallel to our situation today is not obvious. *Theatertanz,* as the title implies, exists in a known tradition, has a narrative element, with a proscenium which promotes an illusion and arouses the audience's imagination. *Theatertanz* uses the tension and resolution of a traditional theatrical context, with movement as the means of progressing the plot and conveying the message. The comparison of podium dance with free dance adds to the confusion. It appears that Böhme equates 'free' with 'free from theatrical traditions'. This implies that podium dance does not aim at illusion or at stimulating the audience's imagination. The kind of words used today for podium dance are the 'plotless dance', 'abstract dance', 'non-literal', 'pure', 'presentational' and 'formalist'. Böhme points out the unsuitability of the traditional theatre space for this genre of dance. He is not alone in this view. By 1930, Gropius from the Bauhaus and Laban, amongst others, had both designed new theatrical spaces for dance and performance art.

Böhme goes on to examine how exactly this new genre of dance communicates to its audience. He decides that rhythmic structure is the primary means of communication but that a theatrical setting is not the best place to appreciate rhythm. He turns to the other tradition of dance, that of participation, and from there to dance as celebration. For us nowadays this is a very restricted view. Rhythmic structure is by no means the only content of plotless dance. However, we need to read Böhme in the context of a time in which dance as celebration was popular and widely practised.

VOL. III, NO. 1, APRIL 1930

At the Turning-Point of the New Dance

Alfred Schlee

A fundamental transformation is taking place in the evolution of German dance. It cannot be denied that a state of artistic stagnation exists. The reason for the crisis lies not only in the financial plight which is badly affecting all fields of contemporary artistic activity. Although this might be aggravating the difficulties, the root cause of the predicament lies more in the uncertainty over artistic questions.

Several years ago, the New Dance had already lost contact with the general artistic development of the day and attempted to keep itself clear of all influences. All living art draws its nourishment from the atmosphere of the time from whence it comes. The current way of thinking determines artistic fashion, and the work of art produces its capacity to remain ever youthful out of perpetual struggle. The tendency, the fashionable mood of art, is like a garment which must be changed frequently. But this tendency only affects the external appearance of the work of art and not its essential nature.

The artistic revolution of Expressionism tried to take things further. The Expressionist artists raised their banner above the purely artistic. They wanted to resume contact with the 'primordial elements of Art', the cult element in primitive artistic practice and the religious aspect of mysticism. Images, speech and music exploded from their usual spheres and became the means to a collective experience of rapturous force. The experience, the ecstasy, were the focus of Expressionist works of art.

The New Dance arose out of this revaluation of artistic principles. It was the most powerful manifestation of Expressionism. The Expressionist artist emphasised the immediacy of the work of art. He abhorred the idea of any kind of intermediary which might thrust itself in between the inspiration and its realisation. His creation is not formed consciously but as a result of submission. For it is not he who speaks but that higher something which reveals itself through him and to which he surrenders. In no other artistic genre could the mystical connection be so intense, the rendition occur so directly as in dance. Here the human being is himself the instrument; there is therefore no need for any further transposition of the initial experience.

It goes without saying that this dance had to take a strong stand against ballet. Quite apart from the fact that ballet in Germany at that time had been at a very low ebb, its sociological structure was also in great contrast to the democratic, revolutionary nature of the New Dance. Ballet has always been purely theatrical, even when it abandoned the framework of sheer performance and became a social event; it always remained visual theatre even when clad in the dress of tragedy. What the New Dance means to us is well known. This is not the place to give a list of the events which led to the peak performances of the New Dance. The fact that these experiences were only occasionally of a purely theatrical nature is clear from the explanation already given.

However, Expressionism and its conception of the work of art was only one stage in the development of present-day art. Certainly it was an important one, but its radicalism can only be understood as a reaction to what went before. The climax of the New Dance movement was reached in its first few years. Its energy was still unbroken, its achievements were magnificent. What is more, one might assume that the spectators were taken more with the concept of the new than with its execution, for which they had no yardstick. Repetition is lessening the impression; variations of presentation are not too great, the emotions continually stir themselves up and the spiritual experience becomes a cliché. The New Dance has been credited with the reawakening of the consciousness of the body and with stimulating a new form of folk dance in the communal dance of the movement choir. Artistically speaking the New Dance has given rise to extremely valuable impulses but it has overrun the mark and is in danger of losing touch with future developments.

It was a mistake to try to construct a New Dance theatre solely from ritualistic elements and it was also a mistake to reject ballet technique simply because its stylistic influence was feared. The New Dance has not been able to devise a new technique which might have replaced that of ballet, and the artistic results of such attempts restricted themselves to works which were not really at all theatrical in character. The New Dance had identified itself with Expressionism, and thus at that moment when Expressionism ceased to be the current expression of the times, it too lost its significance. Another consequence of this alliance was its confinement to German-speaking countries, an isolation which forced its development even further into a cul-de-sac.

The New Dance is obstinate. It does not concede to only having been an episode. (As such its significance is immense.) It is also irresponsible in the way it time and time again produces young dancers with totally insufficient technical training.

However, the transformation and clarification of German dance is already under way. In the theoretical field the means are being created the use of which will facilitate the return to a consciously constructed art of dance. 'Written Dance' brings the consciousness-raising analysis of the method of notation into play in between the artistic inspiration and the final composition. Dance notation has at present a particularly topical significance.

Yet the most recent development of a whole series of German dancers also clearly shows the endeavour to be free from the emphasis on feeling and to retrieve the true nature of dance through the shaped movement. This transformation does not imply any renunciation of the achievements of the New Dance, it merely signifies the retrenchment of all components to their current proportions, namely a clear demarcation between the distinct realms of gymnastic exercise, amateur dance (the movement choir) and art-dance. This realignment necessitates, moreover, a fresh attitude to ballet, which is now no longer the hostile adversary. The direction which Diaghilev has given to ballet in France is a very similar one to the path struck by the most spectacular artistic phenomena in Germany. In some of this company's work there are sections which could have been lifted straight out of German choreography. The 'ballet' technique does not disturb this impression; on the contrary it gives a solid basis to the performance along with a precision which is seldom met with in German dancers. This remarkable coincidence of similar ideas enables us to view the turning-point of the German dance with optimism. This turning-point is the pause before the decisive step which seals the end of the New Dance and which, at the same time, sets the fresh objective; the creation of a European dance.

VOL. I, NO. 2, OCTOBER 1928

Dance in its Time

Lasar Galpern

(excerpt from the book *The Restrained Dance* soon to be published)

We live in an era in which people, in their constant pursuit of records, believe they can neglect to create a meaningful basis for their achievements. They seek to turn the world into a freak-show and attempt to cover up their genuine passion with a desperate search for ecstasy. Should we therefore be surprised if this philistinism affects an art which, in its essential nature, is deeply opposed to any form of frantic activity?

Dance schools are mushrooming all over the country and fashionable young ladies no longer take piano lessons but are going to 'rhythmic gymnastics' classes instead. This is called 'physical culture'; it is, however, merely a form of snobbishness and could easily be disregarded, had it not, because of public opinion, had such a poisonous and dangerous influence on the art of theatre dance with which the public has often confused it. If this newly awakened 'love' for dance had been confined to young ladies wanting to perform in public even though only the most basic gymnastic exercises had been learned, we could console ourselves that, only a generation ago, all girls aspired to be actresses.

Unfortunately, however, this form of amateurism, which is nothing really but a stage of adolescence, has been given the status of an art in our society. A number of writers were only too eager to provide the necessary theories, and no matter how confused these theories were, they helped to bring the 'new dance' into existence.

The reason that such pseudo-intellectual nonsense is treated as a revelation is that the art of dance is not indigenous to our culture. Our intellectuals, who only came of age during the war years, have neither seen a dancer of any importance, nor can they imagine one. Thus they are quite willing to believe that ballet is meaningless and outdated, no matter how little truth there is in that view. What they have not considered is that someone who

9

stammers is not meant to be an actor and therefore someone who has two left legs should not perform as a dancer on stage. In other words: however much one is opposed to the academic rules of ballet, one has to admit that the classical school has produced a degree of physical control that is hardly ever seen elsewhere. Modern dancers are so obsessed with the slogan 'the technical age' that they forget to acquire whatever technique is necessary in order to dance. They content themselves with accusing ballet of unnatural drill and artificiality. What they have tried to promote in place of ballet's emphasis on physical control is the relaxation of the muscles, a form of movement which has been 'freed'. Thus an originally valid idea which neither the classical school, nor Isadora Duncan, nor Jaques Dalcroze had been opposed to, was distorted beyond recognition. However, Dalcroze never had the intention of training dancers, and the classical school regarded relaxation and release only as one of the many sides of dance training.

What we should do is to free ourselves from the rigidity of classical ballet, while keeping its immensely effective method of training the body, and use it in combination with the proven principles established by the more recent dance educators. Thus we should create a sound foundation for a truly contemporary and individually adapted form of artistic dance. What we are doing instead is restricting ourselves to one very limited doctrine.

Relaxation in the context of dance is only a passive aspect of movement; it is hardly suitable for exploring the more sensual side of emotion. The modern dancer, therefore, tries to find a solution through the abstract; she dances *The Evil Rhombus, The Friendly Line*, the *Prelude to a Triangle* and other equally odd compositions. These dances, she claims, contain her entire soul, the spirit of the time, as well as various other important elements, none of which can be identified objectively. For if a dancer waddles along instead of jumping, we cannot be sure if this might not be an expression to show the construction of a triangle. Equally, if a young lady is so relaxed that she would collapse completely were it not for her bones holding her up, we can easily find an explanation by blaming the influence of the 'evil rhombus'.

Of course, we should appreciate that there are also serious people who want to express serious ideas in our present world of dance. But before we agree to start a discussion of such matters we have to make one demand: we must get away from the idea of abstractness in order to experience a healthy and positive form of physical expression which does far greater justice to our newly discovered and widely talked about physicality than the confused feelings caused by undigested metaphysics.

What matters nowadays is the synthesis of a traditional technique with a modern spirit, in the sense that traditional technique provides the basic tools but not the means for expression in dance. A few people have already realised that this is an absolutely essential factor, and more dancers will come to the same conclusion once they stop hiding behind metaphysics. It is only then that we can achieve what so far we have striven for in vain: a modern dance which is lively and in touch with reality – the New Dance.

VOL. II, NO. 1, JANUARY 1929

A Reply to Lasar Galpern's Article 'Dance in its Time'

Berthe Trümpy

A Russian restaurant in Berlin has 'Bitki à la Kosak' on its menu. A bourgeois German man eats it with great devotion, even though it is a perfectly ordinary German beefsteak which he would have normally rejected with great contempt.

This is exactly what is happening with The Russian Ballet at present. In the past, it happened to Italian music.

In Germany, ballet as a technique and as an attitude towards life has lost its status as an art form for almost a hundred years now. The successes of the Russians, however, are falsely attributed to this form of physical training. The true reasons for these successes are completely different. Russians have natural physical ability, Germans do not. In all areas (this applies to music too), Germans make up for their lack of physical talent with intellectual ability. A German's intellect equips him for exceptional achievements. This applies to dance too. However, we cannot expect appreciation from those who lack this specifically German attitude.

The controversy between ballet and new dance reminds me of the dispute that surrounded German and Italian music, in particular the contrast between Beethoven and Cherubini. Beethoven greatly appreciated Cherubini. The new dancers appreciate and admire the qualities in the Russian dancer which are rooted in the genius of that race. Other than that he is of little interest to us.

It is the genius of the Russian race which elevates The Russian Ballet high above all European ballet companies. The reasons for their brilliant performance do not lie in ballet technique. It is important that we finally clarify these misunderstandings.

Pavlova would be an outstanding dancer even without ballet technique. It is personality that counts, not the training of the body.

Ballet as such is not an art; it has nothing to do with art. All attempts to create a synthesis of classical and modern dance are therefore bound to fail. Ballet misinterprets modern dance by copying its techniques of expression only, but not its spirit nor its artistic essence. Acrobatics can never be art. Scales and Czerny *Études* do not belong in the concert hall. Ballet exercises have a certain *raison d'être,* but only as part of the comprehensive training system created by the superior intellect of modern choreographers.

Ballet-dancers overestimate the importance of turned-out feet, pointe work and jumps. Any elephant in a circus could be trained to perform comparable feats. The charisma of a Mary Wigman, however, can only be present if it is based on a form of physical expression which incorporates and transmits deeply felt spiritual and intellectual values.

Exercise sequences as found in modern dance (Wigman's active and passive scales, Laban's directional and spatial swings, etc.) educate the mind as well as the body; they are not only beneficial for the professional dancer, but for everybody.

Previously, piano lessons, though ridiculed by many, were of immense importance for establishing the high level of participation and achievement in music. Nowadays, this is paralleled by the large number of young girls, manual workers and students attending the amateur courses in our dance schools. Dance has grown, as music had previously, beyond small professional circles and has become an important means of development for all mankind. And of course, just as in music, where we find jazz and popular music, there are dance forms which are closer to popular entertainment than they are to art.

'Away from abstractness into a healthy sensuality' Lasar Galpern suggests. Into what? Perhaps into mime which so completely lacks the creativity and imagination dance can offer us? Lasar Galpern fundamentally misunderstands the meaning of abstraction in dance. It frees the dance from elements which are inherently alien to it, such as dramatic, literary, sculptural and other elements. Only when abstraction has been achieved can these elements be re-introduced, but merely to serve the dance and not vice-versa.

To show the character of ballet and modern dance, I am quoting two of their most famous representatives:

> Perfectly fitting shoes are particularly important. But you also have to practice a great deal and observe other dancers to see how graceful they are, then you go and copy them.
>
> (Pavlova)

> The essential themes in dance are the same as in the other performing arts: Man and his fate. In all its variations, from the starkest realism to the most subtle form of abstraction, through its capacity for change, its associations, its struggles, its needs and its solutions, the dance can give a definite shape to every aspect of human life. Man's fate becomes the universal subject for an unlimited and always meaningful number of variations. The dancer, in the first place, is a servant to the work of art.
>
> (Mary Wigman)

VOL. IV, NO. 1, JUNE 1931

Dancing

Valeska Gert

(from a talk given at Radio Leipzig)

Life is too short for me. As it is not in my power to extend it I have to give it depth. This is the reason why I create art. Whatever the artist produces, whether one calls it good or evil, it is all equally important and in a certain sense equally valid. It is ennobled by the creative act itself. There is no such thing as a vicious or evil work of art, it is always subordinated to a higher purpose. Its purpose might be to show that vicious and evil people are merely poor creatures who do not know how to free themselves from their unfortunate predicament.

What place does modern dance occupy in the contemporary history of the arts? Modern dance represents the transition from old to new theatre. The modern dancer had to liberate himself from old theatrical ways and he had to become independent. He did not concern himself with tradition, he was without the constraints of old theatrical conventions. In total naïvety he gave visible expression to his innermost feelings. The directness of expression in modern dance is similar to that of conventional theatre (but not of the ballet). The disassociation from everything superficial, the restriction to essentials created the most intense movement and the most intensive expression possible: the dance. The dancer of our time, if he does not want to stagnate, has to be articulate about his intentions. His only mission is to be the link between the old and the new theatre. His need for expression frequently pushes him to use masks. He wants to say something, and as he is unable to do so by means of his body alone, he uses a mask. Our time strives for the absolute, the typical, the non-personal, hence the mask.

But the mask alone is not enough. The dancer must express his feelings with so much intensity, that the body itself becomes the absolute, the typical: the mask. The theatrical modern dance is not, as often assumed, a modern version of classical ballet but it is a modern development of the theatre, a dramatised moving presentation of modern man.

Now I will talk about my own dances. How I create them varies. Usually I am possessed by a certain tension which can last for days. This tension disturbs me. I try out various movements. If they release the tension, then they are good. I often deliberately make the tension last in order to create the amount of new forms I need. Sometimes I achieve this without effort and in a very short time but sometimes I cannot find movements which release the tension and I work over and over again in my search for them. This tension has become very real to me and I can recreate it whenever I like. Once a piece is made I do not give up until it is perfected, if I believe at all in its development. Some dances remain of interest to me for a long time, some even at the peak of their creation no longer excite me and I abandon them. Often I hear from the audience, 'why don't you do your *Tango* or *Circus* or *Cabaret'*, or one of the others, but if these dances are dead and finished for me I cannot ever repeat them.

My favourite dance is the one I can change the most. What is permanent and never changes is the basic structure of steps and movements. Each time the same steps follow each other in the same order: what is changing, however, is the emotion out of which the dance grows. I experience the dance anew each time. In *Kanaille* (*The Dregs*) a different destiny is presented every time but it is always the destiny of a prostitute. One day this girl enjoys her work, another day she despises it, yet on another day she does her work out of desperation or indifference, or even out of spite. As there is a different emotion behind the dance each time it is performed, the character of the steps changes as well. This makes them appear improvised, the same steps that yesterday were performed with hesitation and resentment the next time are performed quickly and with enjoyment. The climax of this dance is the surrender. In my dance *Der Tod* (*Death*) I always repeat the same phrases: from walking slowly to shouting aloud in fear of death until I gradually let go of life and its anguish and give up peacefully. Only every time my death is different, sometimes my fear is greater, sometimes I surrender more easily. The climax of the dance is my anguish. I am not interested in presenting a particularly artistic arrangement of movements. I only use the most basic and easiest of steps. If one takes the body and its own laws as a starting point, the result will be a dance in which the actions have grown out of each other. However, if one wants to create from the depths of one's spirit and soul, one should not simply develop one movement out of another. Also, I do not believe that by simply devising a skilful sequence of movement one can reveal one's soul. Art shies away from the deliberately 'artistic'. It happens so often that dances are created according to recipes, although even in an activity as functional as cooking, the most beautiful dishes can only be created through an intuitive approach. I believe that art is sorcery; if the spell is successful then the body will follow the mind without resistance.

I have never created thirty jumps and forty turns in succession but I know that I could perform these thirty jumps and forty turns if I felt the need to do so. If sometimes a performance of mine is not a success I do not attribute this to failure of technique but to the fact that I did not immerse myself sufficiently. However, when I do then I can achieve anything. I can paint or make sculptures. In the theatre I can act Medea, the nursemaid in *Romeo and Juliet* or Gretchen in *Faust,* or even Joan of Arc. The training of the body, therefore, takes only a second place. What is most important is the training of the soul. However, this does not happen in measures of space and time.

Figure 1. Oskar Schlemmer: *Triadic Ballet*, 1926 (photo: anon.), in Schlemmer, Oskar *The Letters and Diaries of Oskar Schlemmer*, (ed. Tut Schlemmer, tr. Winston Krisham), Middletown, Conn.: Wesleyan Univ. Press, 1975

Figure 2. Oskar Schlemmer: *Pole Dance*, 1927 (photo: anon.), in Schlemmer, Oskar *The Letters and Diaries of Oskar Schlemmer*, (ed. Tut Schlemmer, tr. Winston Krisham), Middletown, Conn.: Wesleyan Univ. Press, 1975

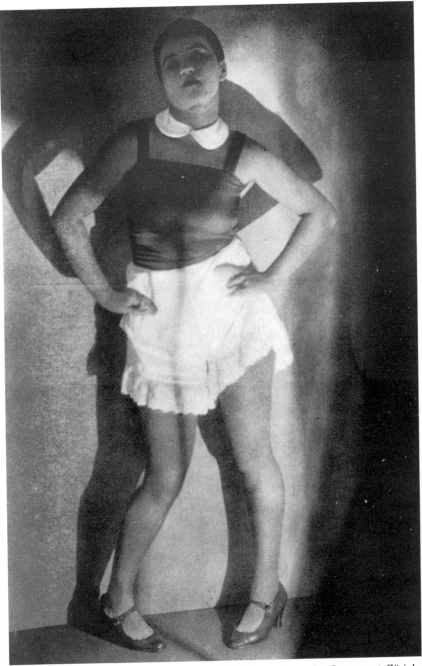

Figure 3. Valeska Gert, 1930 (photo: anon.), in *Tänzerinnen der Gegenwart*, Zürich: Füssli Verlag, 1931

Figure 4. Choreographisches Institut Laban, 1928 (photo: Keystone View Company, Berlin), in Freund, Liesel (ed.) *Monographien der Ausbildungsschulen für Tanz und tänzerische Körperbildung*, Berlin: Alterthum Verlag, 1929

Figure 5. TOP LEFT Choreographisches Institut Laban: Laban and class, clowning, 1927. *From l. to r.*: Dussia Bereska, Gertrud Snell, Ilse Loesch, Beatrice Loeb, Martin Gleisner, Rudolf von Laban, Gert Ruth Loeszer. (photo: anon., Laban Collection)

Figure 6. LEFT Hamburg Movement Choir's Men's Group: *Canon in Space*, 1926. Leader Albrecht Knust (photo: anon., Laban Collection)

Figure 7. ABOVE Hertha Feist's Laban School: *Men's Dance*, 1925 (photo: anon., Laban Collection)

Figure 8. ABOVE Jenny Gertz's Children's Movement Choir, 1926 (photo: anon., Laban Collection)

Figures 9, 10 and 11. BELOW LEFT, BELOW AND OVERLEAF Amateur dancers from Hertha Feist's Laban School in the Berlin Stadium, 1923 (photos: anon., Laban Collection)

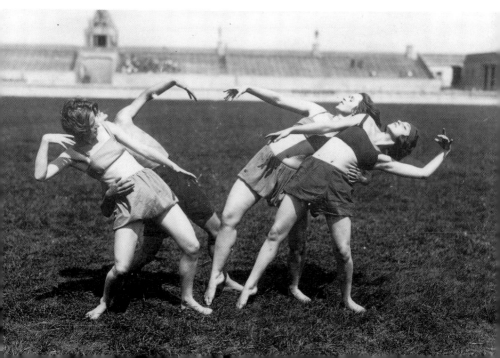

Figure 11. (FOR CAPTION SEE OVER)

Figure 12. Mary Wigman with students in *Dreieck* (*Triangle*), 1930 (photo: anon.), in 'Sie und Er', Nr. 49, 1931

The prerequisite is that a person be truthful. A liar, a false person, cannot create, just as a soul that is twisted has no power.

Dance is movement of the soul that is translated into movement of the body. A dance only needs to consist of a few gestures of the hands, a slowly rocking head, or an arm stretching out. It might need nothing more to be called a dance if behind it we can see the expression of the soul.

In some of my dances my feelings were so intensified that I could barely suppress my screams of pleasure or pain. One day I went further and I did not suppress my screams anymore. Thus for example the *Kummerlied* (*Song of Sorrow*) is an outburst of sound rhythmically arranged. I begin to sob slowly, gradually the sobs become stronger until they peak in painful cries. Then they diminish and the dance ends with short sighs. One day even sound was no longer enough for me and I moved on to words. I created these in the same way as I had created movement. In order to release tension I spluttered out words to myself. Those that seemed to free me I retained and combined together. Thus my 'Diseuse' was created. This process seems to resemble dramatic art. But why, in any case, should dance and drama be divided so strictly? The basis for both is the human being who wants to communicate in movement and sound depending on what the situation requires.

I try to be clear and unambiguous. I like to create order, particularly in my emotional life, by expressing in art what is too strong in real life. If this option were not open to me I would become depressive and indulgent. I also like to create order in my works of art, and therefore I make them as short, clear and unambiguous as possible. Some pieces of mine appear to be comic, some tragicomic or simply tragic. I never know this in advance. A piece that seems to be tragic today may be tragicomic tomorrow. The outcome always depends on my mood. On days when I am cheerful my dances or spoken pieces lose the edges that they had on days when my soul was bitter. No matter how carefully I rehearse a dance, once I perform it on stage it might look completely different from what I had expected.

I am not a solo dancer. I need a partner and this partner is my audience. When I performed in public for the first time people thought I was grotesque. I was satisfied that I fitted into a category. However, I do not feel that need now. For me every dance is a path that I pursue from the beginning to the end, and even beyond into a land which people call fantastic, grotesque or metaphysical. The stage itself is of great importance. The larger the auditorium the smaller the stage should be, for energy is more concentrated in a small space; a small stage increases my expressive powers. However, if the auditorium is small I prefer a large stage as a small auditorium is aggressive to me and I try to escape by having a large stage. The floor, too, is of great importance. Despite the fact that my feet are covered with shoes they can be very sensitive and the right floor covering can improve one's performance. One should only dance barefoot when naked or simply covered in a shirt. A dance costume requires shoes. Whenever I create a dance I visualise the costume at the same time. That is the reason why nobody else can design my costumes for me. I always choose the most simple designs and I prefer pure and clear colours. I was the first artist to introduce brilliant and loud colours to the stage. Recently, however, I have introduced more subtle colours. I only choose simple music for dance. So far I have not used a piece of music that could not be played on any skating rink.

Nowadays many people create art that is not genuine. Talent and creativity alone do not make an artist. There are many ordinary people with talent and there are many artists who not only lack talent but who do not even possess skill. Those people who merely think of themselves as artists usually have a good mind and a certain confidence to express themselves. They have to construct their works, whereas a real artist creates from subconscious powers, and it is only at a later stage that reason comes into play.

I would like to comment on how art relates to a particular period. I believe that any artist can only create in the context of his own period. He is entwined with it. If he fails to do so he is simply indulging in aesthetic games. If an artist penetrates deeply into his time he will uncover its underlying significance and he will also create something that is eternal and universal for all mankind. Some earlier works only appear to be timeless to some people because they were not created in our own era. Our works on the other hand will appear timeless to future generations only if they are profound enough. They will deliver a message which passes from generation to generation and which reveals that we are all human, we all have to follow the same laws, we all have to fight, we all have to die.

VOL. IV, NO. 1, JUNE 1931

Between Ritual and Cabaret
[excerpts]

Ernst Kállai

What I am arguing against is the disastrous tendency of the new dance movement to live above its intellectual means. There is far too much symbolism overloaded with ideas and not enough direct, lyrical or dramatic musicality in dance. Maybe there is a fear of falling back into the pure enjoyment of music as is the case in classical ballet. It is probably also because of a lack of musicality of the body which is far rarer than musicality of the ear. Musicality is not simply a case of matching the movements as smoothly as possible to the music, as in social dance. What I mean is the rare musicality of the dance which seems to be able to take the freedom to wander far from the accompanying tune, without losing the connection to it, simply because the innate link between the two is so secure . . .

There is often a danger nowadays that, as a reaction against ballet's superficial playfulness, dancers overload their art unnecessarily. This also applies to choreography. Oskar Schlemmer's so-called *Raumtanz (Space Dance)* based on Bauhaus principles, is nothing but a structural arrangement of the stage inspired by certain laws of modern painting. The beginning is quite characteristic of these dances. The curtain opens, and we see a stage arrangement based on strict architectural principles; there are various constructions projecting into the stage from all sides, and from below, creating a rigid, tense atmosphere. The dancers are motionless, they are like statues subjected to the strict spatial order of the architectural design. For one second we see a most impressive 'living picture'. But only so far as it remains static. The moment that the dancers begin to move, the unity of the dancers and space, so dependent on the static design, disintegrates hopelessly, unless of course the structural design of the stage changes in accordance with the dancers' movements. This could be mastered quite easily through the use of film projection. But then there is another danger: the dancer might become merely a puppet completely subordinated to the mechanics of space. In this case I would rather see a pure space dance without dancers.

VOL. IV, NO. 2, OCTOBER 1931

Misunderstandings: a Reply to Kállai

Oskar Schlemmer

There are cynics who say that some of the best things in this world happen because of misunderstandings. Should this be the case, it would be dangerous to give an explanation and thus deprive a good thing of its misunderstanding. However, we might be consoled by the fact that the absolute, the ultimate, cannot be expressed in words anyway, at least not in art. What a misunderstanding, to try to capture everything through the use of words.

My stage and choreographic work is resting at present, as I have to fulfill various pleasant and not so pleasant duties as a painter. These are duties that I have to fulfil without an audience: to transform faces into pictures from colour and canvas. Therefore I cannot prove anything in practice by giving an example, which possibly is the only effective way of clarifying a misunderstanding. Nevertheless, I shall use written language to explain how something should not be understood.

In the last issue of this magazine, Ernst Kállai dedicated a few lines to me, misunderstandings that I did not quite expect from him, especially as he spent several years at the Bauhaus in Dessau and thus had ample opportunity to get acquainted with certain ideas. I repeatedly have had the impression that writers, in particular, were predestined to misunderstand visual phenomena; it is as if they saw not through their eyes but through their intellect. Therefore, let us start with Ernst Kállai's confusion. He points out the shortcomings of a highly stylised theatrical form which nowadays is completely antiquated and is rarely seen any more: the curtain opening and the actors or singers forming an almost statue-like beautiful picture which, as soon as the action starts, 'disintegrates hopelessly'. Ernst Kállai also refers to certain Expressionistic stage scenes in which 'various constructions were projecting into the stage from all sides, from above and below, creating a rigid tense atmosphere', scenes which, once the actors start moving, do not disintegrate but remain completely static. I tried, in several essays, to define and to clarify the word 'spectacle', and how, in its purest sense it comes into existence through the movement of colours and shapes alone. Man's only role is that of 'spiritus rector' at the control of the panel from which he directs the entire mechanism. Such a spectacle, to which Hirschfeld's 'experiments with light reflections' could partially contribute, might be called a 'space dance', as the space as a whole is dancing, i.e. it is moved mechanically.

A 'space dance' is what we once called the form of movement theatre which was performed on the Bauhaus's stage. Three geometrical shapes (a square, a diagonal line and a circle) were drawn on the dance floor, and were stepped by three dancers using different tempi and movement sequences. Thus the space itself became intensely expressive, yet this was only due to the dancer's variations in the speed of their kinetic actions. There were no 'static pictures' other than at the end when the three dancers simultaneously arrived at the centre.

Much of what we did was surprising (even to us). One example is when we tried to fix the centre of a space with the use of tightened ropes and the tensions created a completely different sense of space and movement. Another experiment, which had never been tried before even though it seems so obvious, also achieved a surprising result: the use of poles fixed to the dancer's limbs acting as their extensions. The greatest surprise was the movement itself. There certainly was nothing 'static' about it. 'If you have eyes use them' for it must have become clear that mere intellectualising is unlikely to get to the heart of the matter! The fact that the figurines of the *Triadic Ballet* only had meaning when they moved in space, became obvious when we looked at them as motionless exhibits in Paris and Zurich. Even the attempt to rotate them mechanically could not replace the dynamic movement in space for which these figurines were planned. Dancers from the Laban School who initially were suspicious of the costumes, gradually grew accustomed to them and found an increasing number of possibilities for using them with great dynamic power. I would also like to point out that no lesser artist than Mary Wigman showed genuine and unprejudiced appreciation for my ballet. It seems that great artists are so much more likely to recognise the worth of an art, even though it is opposite to their own, than are their students who are often too blind in their fanaticism.

The greatest misunderstandings were created by the terms 'mechanical' or 'mechanistic'. 'Mechanical dancers' was the cheap slogan used to describe the figurines of the *Triadic Ballet*. However, 'mechanical dancers' have quite a different nature from these figurines. They could once be seen in cabaret and variety shows; figures constructed of metal, wheels and various other parts of machinery. Fritz Lang's girl in *Metropolis* fitted into this category. When I created the *Triadic Ballet* all mechanical aspirations were far from my mind, for there was no such thing as a 'machine cult' in 1919. The formal approach I used when making the ballet sprung from basic rules of geometry and stereometry which I translated into new, and contemporary, interesting materials. It also sprang from the anatomy of the human body which, apart from being made of flesh and blood and having a mind and feelings, is also a miracle of biomechanical exactness. If we choose to look at this particular side of the human body, and use it in performance, we are not denying the existence of the other side. All we are doing is creating a balance in a field which is commonly called dance and in which the other side is so immensely over-represented.

I never created a 'mechanical ballet', even though it might be tempting to construct mechanically controlled dancing figures and scenery. Such a relatively restricted scope of movement, however, would not justify the high cost of the machinery. Even the mechanics of the puppet are relative, as the puppet is not an automaton as E.T.A. Hoffman's *Olympia* is, but is moved by the human hand. The puppets of the *Figural Cabinet* are moved and carried by masked dancers: man, therefore, always plays a part.

I readily admit that I came to dance from the fields of painting and sculpture. It is precisely for this reason that I greatly appreciate movement, the essential nature of dance. It is my former field of expression which is static by nature, 'movement that is captured in one moment'. The visual artist's world of form and feeling is highly compatible with that of the dancer, and there is no need to justify crossing from one specialist field to another which so often proves to be a highly fruitful endeavour. What is necessary, however, is that the painter's sensitivity comprises a sense of physicality, which only needs to be awakened in order to manifest itself with vitality and immediacy.

The term 'abstract' also led to misunderstandings. I equate 'abstract' with 'style', and 'style' is known to mean 'final form', the closest to perfection. One has to overcome naturalism (which is not exclusive to painting) and one has to rid the work of art of non-essential accessories in order to achieve the greatest possible precision of an idea. The routes that lead to this aim depend on one's starting point. If I start with the body and gradually develop a form of dance from it, the route is quite different than if I start with a form and use the body simply as a means to its realisation. As the first approach is so much more common, it is in the interest of balance to try the second approach every so often. Whenever that happens and because it happens so rarely, it seems to be an extreme statement, an experiment. There is no doubt that our present time is averse to experiment. Nevertheless, that second approach should not be neglected. When the impulse is strong, when it springs from inner necessity and it is not merely an extravagant passing fashion, only then is it alive and the exact time of its realisation does not matter. For what else is the meaning of experiment if not the next step into the future?

VOL. III, NO. 2, JUNE 1930

Imagination and Experience in Dance
Gaukelei, Drosselbart, Schwingende Landschaft[1]

Fritz Böhme

Art can never be evaluated on its content alone. There will always be the question of the form of a work of art. Each art-work has to serve a certain purpose, and it will be evaluated on the grounds of whether this purpose has been expressed successfully with the help of a specifically chosen form. If someone prefers theatre dance[2] to pure dance, or even values one of them more highly than the other, this evaluation can never be an artistic judgement, because both of them are forms with special purposes. It would be merely an evaluation of these respective special purposes which is being judged, that is of artistic motivation not of art itself. If someone thinks of the theatre in general as being an old-fashioned form of communication, or even as irrelevant to our times, he will consider theatre dance also to be superfluous and even harmful as an art form. Theatertanz does not represent a form determined by 'dance'. On the contrary it is more of a compromise which has its origins in 'theatre'. It is a compromise between the satisfaction of the urge

1 Gaukelei is translated as 'Illusions' and also as 'Jugglery'; Drosselbart is a fairy tale, Schwingende Landschaft is translated as 'Swinging Landscape'.
2 The author is referring to narrative dance or dramatic dance.

for movement and exhibition which comes from within man himself on the one hand, and the appropriate form, which is oriented towards a work of art as we know it, from 'theatre' on the other hand. The rejection or recognition of *Theatertanz* as we know it today, does not affect dance as such but rather the theatre.

It is totally different from the other great dance-performance art of our days, the *Podiumtanz*. The Podium is not an artistic form but a framework. The inner form of the dance is not actually affected by the Podium; therefore the *Podiumtanz* is quite correctly called 'free' dance. The creator of a free dance does not have to be guided by anything, but he has to do justice to his material while implementing the artistic aims set by himself. They become apparent to him through the realisation of the meaning of his work that has been given to him intuitively, and later the realisation of the aims becomes a necessary aspect for the creation of form. Therefore he is not subject to the same formal restrictions that we find in the theatre. There, there is the ballet of the opera which is formal but without content, that means it is nothing but an insertion of movement into the musical opera, or there is danced theatrical-drama. In 'free' dance there is first of all the possibility for real, pure movement-based lyricism; secondly it can create its own epic form; and thirdly, a dramatic form can arise from the dance material. Thus its meaning is the expression of spiritual experience through the artistic material of movement and dance.

At this point I do not want to talk about the limitations which the theatre has because of its architecture, which can only allow certain perspective due to its relief stage; still, it is the only element that the Podium, which is similar in shape, and the theatre have in common. Up to now we do not have a theatre-space which fits dance and its special laws. The essential formal quality given by the properties of the proscenium stage is an intrinsic, and therefore an inevitable, force and above all it concentrates the focus on those individuals who are forwarding the plot.

Theatre implies the consequent distancing of spectator and performers. The one who gives and the one who takes are facing each other, but without the identical spatial spheres which promote a direct form of communication, so enabling the magical-sensual effect of the art material to impose upon the imagination of the spectator. Theatre-art has always to be structured in such a way that it enables the spectator to transform his sensual perceptions (sound, gesture . . .) into certain images. The awakening of such images is fundamentally different, and has to be separated from, spiritual experience of a certain inner, dynamic stirring. Such a magnetising event, which provokes an inner change and transformation, means real identification with the deeper spheres of life. This can only be achieved through a direct arousal of the senses themselves by the art material; watching the movement should motivate the spectator himself to move, and hearing music should make him sing. This is how folk-song and -dance were developed at a primitive level. The transference of such direct arousal always happens through rhythm; it is the force of empathy, the blurring of individuality, the abolishment of separating boundaries that sets off the drive for social interaction. The transference of that power, which transforms something into imagination, always happens with the help of something which is completed through gestures, through something formulated, something which is not changing any more; in short, through something which can be characterised by its striving for an externalised visual nature. For the same reason, *Theatertanz,* as a dramatic force, has a tendency towards mime which is a form of movement completely different from anything that directly arouses the drive for movement. If the *Podiumtanz* wants to convey certain ideas in a dramatic form, it cannot ignore such formalised elements and therefore it will come closer to the theatre of the spoken word. But if it is in its interest to integrate the audience into the dramatic experience on the basis of rhythm, it has to be much more consistent by abolishing the separation between spectator and dancer, and it will also become necessary to arrange the whole thing in the form of a dance-festival in dramatic form.

If we look at three art works, Laban's *Gaukelei,* Jooss' *Drosselbart,* and Mary Wigman's *Schwingende Landschaft,* from this point of view, we come to the following conclusion: the first two belong to the category of dramatic *Theatertanz.* Their content appeals primarily to our imagination. Individual conflicts and actions are presented, sometimes in a more general sense as in *Gaukelei,* which is a dramatic solution of the problem of tyranny. Its form can be described as a juxtaposition of rhythmical and gestural elements. In *Gaukelei,* rhythm and choric gesture are interwoven with the action, which is presented in the form of single dances and mimes, so that we can almost speak of rhythmically enhanced mime in space. In *Drosselbart,* rhythmic group sections are combined with a mixture of dance and mime performed by soloists. Because of these characteristics both compositions belong to the theatre. Mary Wigman's *Schwingende Landschaft,* on the contrary, is a lyrical-epic dance suite which has nothing to do with the theatre. It is neither based upon imaginative elements nor does it address the spectator's cognitive faculties. It is based upon motor-activities and it is not problem-oriented. In comparison it might be called lyrical-epic because it is lacking the confrontational aspect which is necessary for dramatic tension; however, it does communicate through some sort of narrative although this is quite different from the traditional mime-dance. The communication works most of all because of the use of rhythmical monotony. This monotony grows into a formal manifestation of mood and experience because of its inherent emotional force. Nevertheless, there are neither literal, denotative gestures, nor gestures which assert by association. The mood in this framework of the summery, wide plain, was not created by the dancer with the help of a hand gesture providing shade for the eyes, as is done in one of the dances of Prince Jodjana. Instead, the whole rhythmical structure, the movement process as such, immediately arouses the experience of summer and not the image of that experience. The spectator is transported into a certain mood; he is transformed together with the dancer. You cannot compare this to the illusory dramatic-dance of today's theatre, which relies upon the use of imagination and understanding with the help of association and intellect. Instead we have to go back further into history to find something analogous to it. It is comparable to the priest's dance of primitive times, which was watched by the community and which was even experienced by them through the practice of actual rhythmical swinging motion. In those days dance served as the medium for the experience of social unity and as a common ground in order to overcome individualism, in the form of festivals. The main object of all *Podiumtanz* is to join in the dance and it also strives for the resurrection of the festival, whereas *Theatertanz* and theatre as such do not have anything in common with the festival sphere. They would have to abolish the barrier between actor and spectator if they wanted to lead people towards a more active experience of a complete unity, by offering them another way of, and form for, watching and listening.

CHAPTER TWO

Written Dance and Choreology

Editorial II

Laban always gave credit to the many collaborators in his notation system 'Kinetographie', which was presented at the Second Dancers' Congress in Essen in 1928, and subsequently published by Universal Edition.

It had been a long haul. His first experiments were in Paris, soon after 1900, where as a young art student, following the advice of Noverre, he watched people's behaviour in the streets and meeting places of the city, noting down what he saw in a crude symbol system.

In Munich, ten years later, he studied documents on dance notation in the city library and at St Gallen early music manuscripts. He began to see his own experiments as a development of Feuillet's and Beauchamp's work on 'Choreographie'.

Reports of the Laban School in Munich and Zurich, in 1916, refer to a dance notation from which students performed. This would have been one of the interim solutions which he found with the help of his leading student and assistant Mary Wigman. She writes of their daily meetings, she trying out his innovative ideas, he poring over the copious pieces of paper from which she danced.

At this time his search was still focused on finding a spatial harmonic system for dance which would form the basis for the written dance. There is no doubt that at this point he took musical harmony and music's notation as a possible model. Schoenberg's experiments in revolutionising musical harmonic structure, which also influenced its notation, encouraged Laban to pursue that avenue. His other assistant, Suzanne Perrottet, who was an accomplished musician and like Wigman a Dalcroze graduate, was especially helpful to him at this time.

He also took, in these early experiments, the alphabet and written language as a possible model, searching for both the elements and the syntax of the language of movement. It is significant that in his School of Art he taught *Tanz/Ton/Wort* (dance/sound/word) – three arts, two of which already had a symbol system and for one of which he was searching to provide the system.

Over the next ten years, the problem he tried to solve was how to write motion, not only positions passed through, a task which proved to be extraordinarily difficult. All his various solutions up until 1927 – and there are many recorded in *Choreographie* (1926) – retain this hope, but the successful 1928 solution is a compromise.

His prime collaborators after 1919 were Dussia Bereska, whose interests lay in the dynamics and drama of dance; Kurt Jooss, who brought a dancer's and a music student's background to the problem; Sigurd Leeder, with talents as a graphic artist as well as a dancer/performer; Gert Ruth Loeszer, who had clarity of spatial organisation; and Albrecht Knust, a logical thinker, meticulous in method.

The breakthrough came when the group were assembled during the summer school in 1927 after the First Dancers' Congress in Magdeburg. The final decision on how to cope with the problem of writing continuous time was solved. Until then, movements of the arms and upper body were written above the legs and weight, in the body cross, thus:

LA	RA
LL	RL

The decision to write the arms on either side of the legs, thus:

LA	LL	RL	RA

allowed the vertical line to be used for time by extending it as a continuous staff up the page.

Considerable confusion surrounds the word 'Choreographie'. At that time in Germany the word 'choreography' did not have the meaning that it has today, nor did it mean simply the mechanical action of writing in a notation system. It comprised both those and even more – that is, the integration of the principles of movement, knowledge of possibilities and depth of detail which the understanding of a notation stimulates.

Laban's aim went beyond providing a system, which he saw only as a means. Rather, he concentrated on raising the level of dance discourse. This he saw as possible throughout dance theory and dance practice; the aim being to produce dance critics who are able to study a score of the works they review, dance historians whose source material can be notated dances, choreographers who are able to use notation as an integral part of their dance-making process, and dance teachers for whom an analysis of their material – through the principles of notation – can add another dimension to their understanding of their work.

The journal *Schrifttanz,* as a forum, did not separate notation and notating from other approaches to dance discussion and scholarship; neither did Laban's Choreographisches Institut, where all aspects of dance learning were taught. There, alongside the teaching of dance technique and dance history, choreology was introduced as a new discipline, dealing with the study of dance in its own terms, through new methods appropriate to choreology and based on kinetography, eukinetics and choreutics. The latter two, the study of dance rhythm and dynamics, and the study of spatial forms in dance, were named as an alternative to Jaques-Dalcroze's eurhythmics and Rudolf Steiner's eurhythmy. Dalcroze's work, based on musical rhythmic structure, did not provide what Laban sought for dance; namely, an understanding of its own kinetic structures.

Soon, though, a division began between the practising notator and the rest of the dance world. The financial crisis of 1929 caused the move of the Choreographisches Institut to the Folkwangschule under Jooss and Leeder. Eventually, after 1933, with the emigration of Jooss and Leeder with both the ballet and the school, Albrecht Knust found himself isolated and in sole charge of the notation in Germany at the first Tanzschreibstube (Dance Notation Bureau) in Hamburg. Notating was therefore already in danger of becoming a separate activity no longer at the heart of the professional dance world.

Lizzie Maudrik, a ballet-mistress at Berlin's City Opera at that time, and later ballet-mistress after Laban at Berlin's State Opera House in 1934, voiced the more positive response of the dance world to the notation. Her emphasis on both preservation of the dance heritage and improving the quality of new ballet compositions can be compared with the work of one of her younger ballet-trained colleagues, Aurel von Milloss, who attended Laban's Choreographisches Institut.

His professional work as a ballet-master fully incorporated the choreo-logical concepts contained in the syntax of the notation. These new methods enabled him to take a structural approach to choreography to complement his imagination, thus leading him to change, elaborate, harmonise and make dissonant his ballet vocabulary. Maudrik recognised how notation could assist ballet, while Laban and Milloss saw new horizons for dance composition.

Fritz Klingenbeck, a Laban assistant and later a ballet-master and theatre director, was one of the first expert notators. He pinpoints the issue which began to emerge from notating practice; namely, the distinction between the structure of the work and the performance of that structure. A similar topic is well discussed in linguistics under *langue* and *parole,* or structure and utterance. All writers of dance at this time presumed that movement was the sole dance medium and that in writing the movement they had documented the dance. The fact that the dancer is part of the medium is touched upon in Klingenbeck's article, but only in terms of the dancer's performance of the movement. The contribution to the dance work made because of the physical features of the dancer himself and the impact of his personality were not yet noted, nor was the correlation of sound and movement. Nor were the space, set and costumes mentioned as essential ingredients in the documenting process.

The other early notators were Sigurd Leeder at the Jooss/Leeder School; Albrecht Knust, who with Azra von Laban (Rudolf von Laban's daughter) opened the Hamburg Tanzschreibstube (Dance Notation Bureau); and Susanne Ivers, who was the first notator employed as a professional by the Berlin State Opera when Laban became ballet-master in 1930, and whose scores still exist.

Knust's article is not included in full but is important in that it shows how quickly and how readily Laban's basic principles were developed by his pupils and colleagues. It also shows how meetings where large group works were rehearsed and performed with several amateur groups were important to the development, practical use and dissemination of notation.

Knust's detailed and clearly thought-through article would make difficult reading for readers who are not notators. The 1932 publication of this orthographic contribution from the new Hamburg Dance Notation Bureau formed the basis for the section on group paths and formations in the standard textbooks on Laban's notation published and used in the 1980s. Beginning with his work on group movement notation, Knust became the world leading scholar of Laban's notation and remained so, notwithstanding the refinements made by Sigurd Leeder for writing dance style and the later contributions by his pupil Ann Hutchinson in the USA.

Schrifttanz included several articles on choreology which have not been included in this book as they make heavy and technical reading. In three of them Gertrud Snell discussed elements from the curriculum of the Choreographisches Institut, where she was a teacher. Entitled 'Choreology', 'Choreutics' and 'Eukinetics', in them Snell discussed movement itself from the point of view of a general analysis, a specifically spatial analysis and then an attempt at the dynamics of motion and its connection with expression. Another article we chose not to include was a second paper by Fritz Klingenbeck. He traced how Laban's theory of a harmonic organisation of the spatial forms of dance developed out of the innate harmonic structures in ballet. This was shown especially in the five positions of the feet and their relationship with forward-backward, diagonal and sideways directions, and the forms drawn in space by *port de bras, battements* and *rond de jambes*. His article is in part repetitive of some of the other translated material on the relationship between ballet and the new dance.

Snell's and Klingenbeck's work is important in that it shows the state of understanding at that time of what was to become Labananalysis in the 1950s to 1970s and has now been subsumed within the larger area of choreological studies.

Martin Gleisner was a strongly socialist advocate of 'dance for all' who successfully ran movement choirs for young workers, notably in Jena and Gera. The movement choir was a unique phenomenon of German culture at this time, initiated by Laban. The singing choir, the speech choir and the movement choir paralleled each other, all three with socialist participants. Gleisner co-operated with Bruno Schönlanke, the 'Red' speech choir poet, on many occasions. He created a work entitled *Red Song,* and was associated with the Workers' Movement, using as subject matter for his movement choirs topics which were drawn from the concerns of the 'working masses'. Not all movement choir works were so politically slanted. Laban's *Lichtwende (Solstice)* and *Schwingender Tempel (Swinging Cathedral)* were more poetic, his Viennese *Festzug der Gewerbe (Procession of the Guilds)* was celebratory in character.

Gleisner's article is interesting beyond the question of written dance and amateur dance because of his assertion that amateur dance needed specially created dance works. In fact this need was beginning to be fulfilled by several young dance makers. Lola Rogge is an example of a young dancer who had started her training with the Hamburg Movement Choir and became its leader. Her works, such as *Die Amazonen,* lifted the expectations for the amateur dancer's ability much higher than before. They demanded technical mastery as well as participation and involvement. Without dance works, movement choirs – and indeed amateur or community dance generally – very readily resorted to rhythmical exercise of a calisthenic nature. Laban, Gleisner, Albrecht Knust in Hamburg, Ilse Loesch in Latvia, the Pierenkämpers in Mannheim, Herta Feist in Berlin – to mention only the main choir leaders – fought hard and long to establish the principle of composed and written 'art works' for amateurs, but the National Socialist movement, by 1936, brought their hopes to an end by attempting to use the movement choir for its own political ends.

VOL. I, NO. 1, JULY 1928

The Editorial to the First Issue of *Schrifttanz*

Alfred Schlee

Never before has there been such a surge forward in the art of dance, enabling it to finally find the wide recognition it deserves as a self-contained art form, on a par with music and the other arts. Dance has even become fashionable and is already, if one follows its development closely, in danger of losing momentum. What is the reason for this?

Not every dancer is creative! And improvisation based on feeling, by a dancer not creatively endowed, is not a work of art. Not every dance inventor is a performer. There are creators and interpreters. But the reality and the value of the dance vanish with the death of its performers, if the work has not been captured by a script. All historical attempts to find a dance notation have remained incomplete, for no one had succeeded in coming to grips with the movement of the whole body. It is only now, with the present level of research in physics and biology, that a complete dance notation can be provided.

Today this notation is available. The movement towards dance literacy is grouped around Rudolf von Laban. In his circle kinetography (movement notation) was developed. A step in the development of mankind is thus attained, comparable to the impact of the alphabet on the art of words and the laws of harmony and a system of music notation on the art of sound.

Many questions arise, on the one hand from the effect on dance itself of the creation and the development of dance documentation, on the other hand from the effect of a notation on music, theatre, etc., and these will be looked at by this quarterly journal.

One can already say that the publishing of a specialist journal is undoubtedly justified from the importance of the many-sided nature of these problems.

Therefore the particular wish of the publishers is to provide in the journal a lively exchange of opinions from all those interested in dance notation. Individuals are hereby invited to participate. All suggestions relating to the development of kinetographic publications and of the journal itself, all new and fruitful ideas will gladly be given space in a paragraph specifically designated for the exchange of views.

VOL. I, NO. 1, JULY 1928

A Chapter from the History of Written Dance

Fritz Böhme

Between the first drawing to indicate the direction of a step in the 1605 edition of Caroso's *Ballarino* and the first attempts by Blasis in the 1820s to include the whole body by looking at its gestures, there lie two significant advances in the history of dance. These are Feuillet's *Choreographie* of 1700 and Noverre's *Lettres sur la danse* of 1760. Feuillet's notation is an attempt to give permanence to the most fleeting of all arts by going into extreme detail with the help of drawn sketches. The second work is an attempt to anchor the art of dance deeply as a work of the spirit or intellect and, when anchored, to examine it in conjunction with all the other arts and intellectual activities of mankind. In the first work there is the conviction of having overcome the final obstacle which excludes this art from the others (by writing it down), while Noverre asserts that this conquest is impossible and, in any case, is unnecessary, as it misses its purpose.

Noverre's 13th chapter is devoted to 'choreographie'. And he starts this chapter with the scornful remark: '"Choreographie" is the art of writing down dance with the help of various signs, as one notates music with notes – with the difference that a good musician will decipher two hundred beats in an instant, whereas an excellent choreographist will not decipher two hundred dance beats in two hours.' But Noverre admits that notation may have been necessary at the early stages of ballet, where it was a matter of explaining principles. Then, everything had been clear and simple, and so the notation of steps and floor patterns would have been equally uncomplicated. As far as his own period was concerned, however, Noverre did not believe in the necessity, nor even in the possibility of notating dances. The steps were too complicated, they had doubled and trebled, their combinations were infinite; and even if somebody were able to write them down, the result could not be deciphered by anyone else. Notation contributed nothing at all to the perfection of the art of dance. It certainly could not raise the dancer above what he was. And even if he, Noverre, possessed the most beautiful collection of the best dancers of the standard of a Dupré, of Camargo, and others, he still would only have an incomplete shadow of past realities, a cold and silent copy of the inimitable original.

Although Noverre fought strongly (in such words) against notation, the periods before and after him were inspired again and again by attempts to capture dance graphically. Among these Feuillet's notation was the first which signified a great step forward in the solution of this extremely difficult problem. It should be regarded as the final crowning of the overall achievements made in seventeenth-century dance. For it was during the seventeenth century that the first great attempt was made to create a form of art, a theatrical form of dance with social dance as its foundation. It was no longer merely a matter of steps, but of the entire human form and its motion. Indeed, Antoine Arena and Jean Tabourot during the fifteenth and sixteenth century already used dance notations; they were very simple notes of steps with the help of letters. Something new began to stir when, in the beginning of the seventeenth century, Caroso was the first in the history of dance to go beyond this notation by letters. We know from old sources that Beauchamps was nominated by Louis XIV as Director of the Academy of the Art of Dance in 1662 for his completion of Tabourot's *Orchésographie*. What he contributed that was new to notation we do not know. But we do know that in 1682, in his treatise *Des Ballets Anciens et Modernes,* Ménestrier did not yet contribute anything comparable with Feuillet's notation. It is indeed true that he no longer used the letter notation of the sixteenth century when he recorded his ballets, indicating instead the changing positions of groups of dancers in space. Nevertheless, for him, the concept of horizontal movement was still of such prime importance that he completely ignored the vertical movement of the body, nor did he mention the dance positions and their variations for the individual dancer.

Feuillet, too, still emphasised the line of locomotion; but it must be regarded as a substantial advance, that in addition to this line he described the manner in which the body itself moved. His treatise is an instruction manual for the notation of dance. He starts with the simplest elements in that he gives signs for the dancer, signs for the line of locomotion, for right and left, and other signs. Then follow, according to the code of classical ballet, details of the five positions, of steps, jumps, arm movements, knee movements, and the position of the head. A picture of the entire dance arises from these signs which are placed to the right and left of the line of locomotion, on which the timing is indicated by strokes for the beats. Written dance is no longer a matter of merely handing down a few stereotyped and already existing combinations of steps as was the case in the sixteenth century. Also, the emphasis lies no longer exclusively on horizontal aspects. Written dance has now become a combination of the horizontal, i.e. the line of locomotion with the differentiated movements of the individual dancer. And indeed here was the possibility to record the elements of the dancer's movement beyond the stereotypes, taking into account their differentiated forms. (The basis, however, was always the most beautiful arrangement of steps possible which simultaneously was a symbol for the dancer's aesthetic values of this period.) What we have to recognise is that here is an attempt to capture the individuality of creation. And one must add that, so far as this individuality fitted into the wider aesthetic of ballet with its principles of correct form, Feuillet's *Choréographie* was a great achievement and a work of genius which succeeded in notating dance with the help of graphic signs.

Fundamental changes were only effected in the nineteenth century, when the movement of the body and the line of locomotion were no longer treated as one. The individual movements of the dancer were now being emphasised to a greater extent than had been the case with Feuillet. One looks at the methods of notation such as Saint-Léon's or Zorn's which record the dance profoundly by juxtaposing the movements of the body with the path of locomotion added at the side, and one can recognise that here again there is an emphasis on the individual movement of the body. And this manner of notating extends into the twentieth century. Only now have new principles arisen which start from an entirely different viewpoint to that of Feuillet. The aim now is a union of locomotion and individual movement, hence a union of horizontal and vertical forms.

VOL. I, NO. 1, JULY 1928

Basic Principles of Movement Notation

Rudolf von Laban

Kinetography or movement notation has two objectives, which need to be clearly distinguished.

The first objective is the capturing of movement sequences and dances. The advantages of such a possibility are easy to see; they have been recognised for centuries and have been continually sought, through experiments with varying degrees of success.

The other objective is, from a conceptual point of view, far the more important. It deals with defining the movement process through analysis and thus freeing it from the kind of vagueness which has made the language of dance appear unclear and monotonous.

The first clear difference which can be perceived in the movement process reveals itself through observing the movement flow (time rhythm) on the one hand separately from the movement shape (space rhythm) on the other.

The time rhythm is shown linearly by longer and shorter lines which correspond to the relative duration of the movement. For example:

████████████ ███ ████████████ ███ ███ ███████████

By grouping these in relation to a central line, each individual movement of the right and left halves of the body can be clearly specified and so can the individual limbs (see the system's manual *Methodik der Kinetographie Laban*).[1]

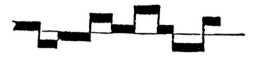

In the linear diagram above, a monolinear movement is shown in which one limb or body part after another comes into action. However, several limbs can function simultaneously, and then a very different kind of polylinear movement expression makes its appearance.

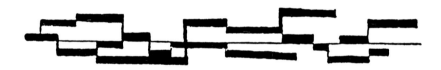

Moreover, the polylinear flow has different expressive possibilities, in that at one time an absolute simultaneity occurs and at another time there is an

overlapping of durations of the individual movements of the limbs.

If one takes these signs, which show the respective duration of the movement flow and how it is performed by the individual body parts, and adds also a directional element, the result is spatial subdivision or, better expressed, the picture of the spatial rhythm and the directional harmony which provides the equilibrium in space of the movement.

1 Published by Universal Edition concurrently with the first edition of *Schrifttanz*.

For this purpose, all that is necessary is three symbols, or rather three variations of the duration block.

These blocks, placed in different ways, enable all spatial directions to be indicated and also deviations, curves and loops in the relevant direction.

In the same way as we can distinguish between monolinear and poly-linear styles, we find further variety in movement styles through the variable combinations of stable-dimensional and labile-oblique directions. These directional combinations arise from being taken into the same direction or in opposition. This forms the basis for a many-faceted dance notation which allows for all the possibilities of the dance language.

A few punctuations and expression signs complete the notation; they describe elements which either restrain or promote the flow and plasticity of the movement.

The final artistic objective of kinetography is however not a notation system but dance literacy.

VOL. II, NO. 2, JULY 1929

Written Dance and Ballet

Lizzie Maudrik

A large part of a ballet-master's responsibilities arises from circumstances of a purely practical nature. The individual has to impart information to a group thus acting as a teacher, as well as having to arrange that group in the function of director. Indeed, there is no other artistic discipline in which the services required from a leading personality extend over so wide a field as is the case of the ballet-master. He actually has to lower himself from being a completely independent artist to being a mere technician who has to rehearse the *corps de ballet*. Certainly, the final product of a ballet often bears the stamp of mere technical exercise. The reason may be that the ballet-master's abilities do not extend beyond technique, or that even though his initial idea had originality, it then suffered during the process of transmission to the dancers. In any case, even taking account of the total unproductiveness of the *corps de ballet,* we have to ask if the ballet-master's mechanical drill-like approach to rehearsals has caused classical ballet to be brought to the dead point at which it undeniably is today.

At this point I want neither to set up 'interesting' hypotheses about possible reasons for the development of ballet, hypotheses which can never be verified, nor do I want to repeat well-known platitudes. One could, however, get far more closely to the core of the matter by asking about the connection between the previously mentioned problem and the significance of dance notation for ballet. The answer will be found easily: a really enormous significance. One can seek for an example in more familiar fields and find it without difficulties in music: how would the performances of choral musical creations be possible if the composer were having to rely on the verbal instruction of each individual musician, or of groups of instrumentalists performing in unison? What consequences would such conditions have, firstly, for the whole work, and secondly, for the creator? The creative repertoire would have to be restricted to absolute essentials, a reduction instead of extension, mechanisation of the dance creation itself instead of development, a freezing, a standing still. Where would the art of sound be, if there was no written music, if the art of sound were not based on the notation of sound? Considering this we must feel boundless admiration for the achievements of ballet which some of us have had the opportunity to see for ourselves and some have been told about. However, we cannot take this comparison any further, without the danger of ignoring the inherent differences in the nature of each of the two art forms. Indeed, there have always been attempts to record dance movements graphically; practically every ballet-master has worked out a system of dance notation for his own needs, in order to aid his memory. However, a proper dance score as such has never existed; no solo or group dancer has ever worked on an artistic project by studying his role independently. And, furthermore, a choreographic (dance writing) achievement has never before found the kind of general appreciation which even the simplest dance production has been certain of for centuries. For a dance is indivisibly connected with the group which performs it and with the leader of the group which created it. In contrast, a piece of music is written down, printed and, whenever an opportunity of performance offers itself, people can listen to it and show appreciation.

There is another related development which from our point of view cannot necessarily be appreciated as progress: the artist who is capable of conceiving great ideas in dance might fail because of the difficulty of bringing these ideas to their fullest realisation, because of the difficulties of successfully imparting them to the dancers who work with him and for him.

Wherever the choreographer cannot find a dancer who is capable of interpreting his work or is not satisfactorily trained as a dancer, he is likely to dance the part himself, in order to express what he has not been able to give objective form to.

Thus we see the ballet-master as principal dancer in the centre of the classical production of ballet companies. His performances stand out more and more, the *corps de ballet* moves further into the background, in fact, it often hardly has even a supporting role. The great stars of the classical ballet are alone or with a partner closely linked to them because of the nature of the work, and only they produce something of great artistic value, with the help of, or in spite of, their technique.

These retrospective analytical observations are unrelated to the historical development of dance, so far indeed as this development is known to us. They do, however, enable us to understand the implications which are inherent in written dance, which touch the ballet as well as the art of dance as a whole, and which will have an influence on its innermost nature. They reach far beyond what, at first sight, simply seems to be a logical, superficial convenience.

Besides the obvious advantage, that the dance composer would thus have the possibility of recording his work of art in the clearest and most logical manner, there is another strong argument for dance notation. It would hasten the development which has already begun, which aims to restore the autonomous status of the work of art after a period of excessive individualism. Thus the following prospect becomes apparent concerning the dance elements of the rather difficult movement sequences which compose ballet (i.e. a *pas-de-bourrée* or a *pas-de-chat*). A carefully worked-out form of dance notation, however, makes it possible to split up these movement sequences into their basic components. These basic components, found analytically, can then be synthesised again, even by changing and newly combining them, and thus new movement sequences are created. Thus, by a purely practical factor, a developmental procedure in ballet is arrived at, which otherwise would advance only very slowly or not at all.

This procedure could attain its goal in only one step. To what unexpected renaissance of the ballet with its wealth of movement motifs, full of brilliant precision, could this self-fertilisation lead? The use of an innovation which at first sight seems to have a purely practical nature, actually gives new life to an art.

Dance is a delight for our eye; it captures our spirits, causes our souls to resonate, and disappears like a sound, nothing remains. We, the audience, retain it in our memory, but the generation following us knows nothing of it. Something of infinite value and beauty is lost forever because of a missing link, because a reliable guardian, an archivist of our thoughts, cannot be found. This is where dance notation can help us, by using all possibilities of a script at once: using calm and realistic methods of comparison and evaluation, it sifts the chaff from the wheat. The choreographer makes several copies of his work, and passes it on; it is being read and judged, it becomes completely independent of its creator, it is performed where it is appreciated. Just as the musician obtains total clarity about a composition from the study of a score, so, with a dance score, a true basis is provided for the objective evaluation of a dance, which could, especially for the dance critic, make his responsibilities easier, and eliminate the subjectivity which, at present, is often quite deplorable.

One more question of great importance emerges here: it is now much more possible to protect our artistic work in a legal sense. According to the Imperial Law of 19 June 1901, which concerns the copyright of literature, dance, pantomimes, and choreographic works are also protected: 'however, they only enjoy protection if the dramatic action is recorded in writing; those written directions for performance which outline the development of the action are sufficient'.[1] One does not need to be a lawyer to understand the inadequacy of this concept and how it does not do justice to the choreographer's achievements. But the fact that the substance of the artistic work of the dancer, and the need to protect it by the law, has not sunk more deeply into the consciousness of the legislator than the 'recording of the dramatic action', the purely superficial development of the action, is solely based on the fact that, even now, the artistic work of the dancer has not yet found a way of being recorded objectively! Once this has been altered and if authorship can be proved by means of a universally recognised dance notation, then the law has automatically deepened its meaning, it has gained precision as a defensive and offensive weapon.

However, I have also shown the problem which has to be solved as a prerequisite by us dancers alone; that is the general recognition, or what in practical terms means the same, the efficiency of a dance notation. I think the basis can be found in Rudolf von Laban's choreography,[2] since it builds on laws which are entirely generally valid and neutral, and from which any movement, however complicated, can be reconstructed in a simple way.

1 Stenglein, *Commentary.*
2 Here in the sense of notation.

VOL. I, NO. 2, OCTOBER 1928

Dance Composition and Written Dance

Rudolf von Laban

I often hear the anxiety expressed that the written dance could endanger the originality of the dance invention. Naturally this can be the case for a number of dilettante dance creations, but these we want to exclude purposely from the artistic business of dance. Mawkishness and intellectual construction are the great dangers for the further development of this art. Both will no longer be possible, that is will not be acceptable, if dance compositions are available which are truly worked out, and if the feeling of the dancers and of the public for actual dance language has been awakened. And that can only happen through dance literacy.

People will now ask, what should be the actual process of the composition in a notated work. That is very simple! In the fundamental nature of the idea of a dance and its development, nothing at all is altered. Like every other artist, the dancer has the desire to communicate an idea arising from his inner life. Only this does not occur in words, in three-dimensional shapes, or in painting, but in a means of expression which is the dancer's own, that is in the movement of one or more human bodies. This movement has elements of rhythm in time and rhythm in space, which, arranged in a particular way, give expression to his experience. Up till now, each dancer, in the arrangement or composition of his experience, has tried to fix these rhythms by practice or repetition, and almost every one, even if he produces only a little, will have to make some notes for himself about this arrangement, so as not to forget it. So one will draw out the paths schematically, another will note down for himself the rhythms, a third will make sketches for himself in words of the content of the events in his dance, etc. Very often the musical score 'reminds' him of the sequence and arrangement of his experiences. Then by continuous improvement a more or less sufficient and clear product of this procedure of invention is established as the final form of the dance. This should remain the case in future, only a properly thought out kinetography provides a quite excellent basis. It assists in the creative work towards a more precise movement statement and enables the completed composition to be established finally and clearly. Both in detail and overall style, the creative dancer will have his product always clearly before his eyes and will be able to judge where and for what reasons any lack of clarity or conflict in style is apparent. Often it proves to be a virtuoso action of the body that distorts the direction and balance of the work, which the composer will easily discover and simplify. Or the exact opposite will occur; the body ought to be dynamic for the development of a splendid and exceptional movement idea, and what actually arises in practice is only a poor use of this accented moment. Here, if the correct proportion and the correct form is found, that is the form corresponding to the dancer's idea, the performer will have to be trained until he can make this form visible. Thus, for the performing dancer as well, the writing down of the composition is both a stimulus and a controlling means for his abilities and for his temperament, which a developed art of the dance cannot be without.

But a dancer who has neither learnt the basics of the possibilities of movement combination nor the basics of the written score, is and will remain an amateur. It would be best if he abandons his experiments, because he only confuses and undermines rather than promotes the general worth of the art of dance. This is equally true of so called 'stars', for sooner or later the emptiness and one-sidedness of their display of temperament become apparent, and the image of the entire art suffers from it more than it does from the pathetic attempts of the hopeless dilettantes.

There is, indeed, always literate dance at work. Everything which is supported by any tradition is quasi-written. The fixed formula of ballet expression, Italian and French ballet, should absolutely be regarded as literate dance, which is nevertheless un-free, restricted and, in terms of the body, ossified. Likewise, the so-called New Dance is a one-sided literate dance of this kind, with its forms based on traditions (some more conscious than others): Greek (Duncan), or oriental (St Denis, Sent Mahesa, Mary Wigman), partly also The Russian Ballet. However, these traditions are based on natural rather than artificial forms of the body. They are somehow richer than the Baroque stylisation of the old western ballet, and thus are a step on the path to a New Dance. The new literacy should bring release from a reliance on these separate traditions, in that it offers an awareness of all the possible movement combinations, whatever they might be as material for dance expression. The way to the realisation of this is a struggle. But happily it is a fact that all honest dancers see the value of this means, even if it is only to record their traditionally styled combinations. Some of them will then slowly arrive at free composition, and thus really attain the value and purpose of the written dance.

VOL. III, NO. 3, NOVEMBER 1930

What Should one Write Down and What not

Fritz Klingenbeck

Something has already been said earlier in this publication about the practical use of dance notation. In the writing of dances, the notator is easily tempted to write in more detail than is useful to the reconstructor. Of course, we have learnt that through notation we can record each movement of the body, however small. This fact has great advantages, above all it provides the utility of a script, and it can also give the numerous movement events which must be followed absolutely in detail. In the writing down of dances, however, things appear to be a little different. The dance notator must, along with a trained eye for the rapid perception of movement events, possess above all an understanding of the actual elements of the dance movement. In this consideration three factors stand out as particularly important, which the dance notator must be able to keep apart reliably. First the actual composition, the naked, clear structure of the dance, second the performance, the personal interpretation of the artist, and third there are in most cases the factors determining style. It may not be entirely simple to draw the boundaries between these three factors, especially between the first two, the composition and the interpretation. Since at present we have still only a small number of notated compositions in existence compared to musical or literary compositions, the writing down of already created dances is the main consideration. It should be assumed that this work will be ongoing in the future. For this reason it may be perhaps worthwhile to consider in detail the differences between composition and interpretation.

It is not necessary to emphasise that guidelines about performance which are given by the choreographer, and are valid for all interpretations of a work, are not included under interpretation. But what is equally clear is that, for the written recording of dances, the individual interpretation of an artist should be much less important than the actual composition. For reconstruction only the latter is considered, for we find only the composition in the written recording of all other arts. The expression of personal performance is scarcely possible with signs or words, it is the unrepeatable, unique possession of the living artist, a peculiarity which we can at best capture with gramophone and film. But the objective of the notation score must be to provide the bare composition for the reconstructing artist, the enlivening must be left to him to create afresh. Then descriptions of performances by others cannot be a disturbing influence on him. Thus, shadow movements do not belong in scores for reconstruction. Thousands of small movements, phrasings, head, feet, are mainly ideosyncracies of the performing artist, for whom it would be absurd to prescribe something else. Thus there falls on the dance writer the same difficult and responsible task, namely to strip away all these secondary manifestations from his notation score and to leave them out of consideration. To recognise what must be written down, and what not, is not entirely easy, because the boundaries are always fluid and in most cases it is exactly the secondary manifestations belonging to the interpretation which can make a dance interesting and valuable. Nevertheless, composition and interpretation must be clearly separated from each other by the dance notator, if another artist is to be able to recreate thereafter.

The third, the factor determining style, is again not to be confused with the interpretation, and hence needs to be treated differently. This factor determining style is not to be found in all dances. For example, many dances by Wigman, the *Wellesz March* by Kratina, and above all dances such as those by Jodjana have those wholly characteristic and often-repeated flourishes, which give rise to certain tensions and postures which are absolutely connected with them. To simplify the writing down of those dances, one can just write down once that typical tension, posture and the associated often-repeated movement flourishes in advance of the actual notation. This single pre-sign indicates the style of the following dance. There is a similar function in music notation, in the indication of keys through '♯' and 'b'. The pre-sign 'b' has already been introduced in the dance notation for the generally recognised expression 'ballet style', and there are others. In this way the writing down of dance will be substantially simpler and clearer, for those factors determining style occur in the notation score as small repetitions which can take up time and detract from legibility. Of course, later in the score, cancellation signs can be used if the pre-sign no longer applies.

These suggestions are directed especially at the emergent dance notators who are over-conscientious and who from time to time despair of their excessive detail. But it should be assumed that professional practice in the direction indicated will reveal many further useful possibilities.

VOL. IV, NO. 1, JUNE 1931

Contributions to the Orthography of Movement
[excerpts]

Albrecht Knust

Schrifttanz editor

Two years ago Albrecht Knust added a bureau for dance notation under the direction of Azra von Laban to his Hamburg Movement Choir, and gave himself the task of thoroughly incorporating notation into practical work. In this case the notation would be placed primarily at the service of the movement choir, of group dance. Inevitably in this connection new problems arose of an orthographic nature. With expert understanding and feeling, Knust has found clear solutions to these problems, problems which sooner or later will confront every notator. In the *Contributions to Orthography* which are now complete, Knust evolves his work with the aid of examples, the results of which deserve to be generally adopted, a fact which is confirmed by Rudolf von Laban's certification that it is suitable for use in notating. At the same time, in his discussion Knust offers several very interesting possibilities of form from the field of group dance, which also deserve to be noted, and given attention. The following observations give a concisely collected overview of the contents of Knust's work.[1]

Albrecht Knust
These *Contributions* are answers to questions which have arisen in kineto-graphic practice and relate essentially to the way of writing group move-ments. The object is, of course, to describe clearly and with simple symbols those phenomena of group dance which keep recurring. These symbols did not need to be invented anew, but were able to be developed from the existing possibilities of Kinetography Laban. Thus they are not a set of new symbols.

The first heading 'Floor Patterns' is to be regarded as a preamble for the later discussions in this paper. The rules inherent in circular paths dealt with there are valid for both solo dance and for group work. They can be condensed into two laws.

Valerie Preston-Dunlop adds:
Knust proceeds to state two laws in fairly stark mathematical terms and he continues by explaining, in detail, the various regular group forms and group pathways which had emerged in the practice of movement choirs and for which Knust found the writing rules. This may also have been one of the first times that the logic of the notation developed possible moves which were then realised in movement choir practice.

Knust gives a second heading, 'Group Pathways', and describes, in technical detail, the group movements for which the following terms were adopted: 'wheeling', 'whirling', 'shifting', 'following and leading'.

For his third heading he describes two kinds of canon, the well known 'canon in time', and the less known 'canon in space' and ways in which their variants might occur and might be written. He then details the 'paths of individuals': spirals, ovals, figures of eight, loops, and continues into the technicalities of groups turning to have different fronts related to a central focus, changing into having a common front such as a proscenium arch. He continues by describing group forms which contract and expand, towards a centre and away from it, and discusses how such a centre might be chosen

1 The following were published by the Hamburger Tanzschreibstube:
    (i) *Vorschläge zur Notierung von Gruppenbewegungen mittels der 'Kinetographie Laban'*, **I** (May 1931)
    (ii) *Vorschläge zur Notierung von Gruppenbewegungen mittels der 'Kinetographie Laban'*, **II** (December 1932)
    (iii) *Beiträge zur Orthographie von Bewegungen*, **I, II, III, IV** (1932)

and written. He deals with questions of how to describe the arrival shape, or destination, of a group movement, of how to describe the movement itself and how these two methods function together in a score and in composition. Finally he touches on how the relationship of two groups might be written, by paying attention to the manner in which they pass, meet, part, and penetrate each other.

VOL. I, NO. 2, OCTOBER 1928

Written Dance and Amateur Dance

Martin Gleisner

If the recent upsurge in the art of dance is not to be left hanging in mid-air and not to fizzle out from a lack of blood, if it is to become more than the concern of experts and less the concern of variously knowledgeable aesthetes, then the dance must be loved, understood and above all practised by the whole public at large. The fulfilment of this demand should not only be sought for dance and for artistic reasons but also for the sake of people and their complete humanity. The education of a person is not harmonically complete, the balance between spiritual forces, feelings and will is not achieved until he has found a worthy form of activity for those shaping forces of his bodily movement which demand expression. This is similar to the way that universally loved, read and spoken poetry, widely heard, played and sung music are other manifestations of his desire for expression.

In relation to this need sport, gymnastics and rhythmic exercise do not suffice because they are all preparation of the instrument, problem-solving exercises, at best purposeful competition. It is only dance that can be an equal human language – like poetry and music are in their spheres; not the everyday form of social dance, but the widely supported Artistic Dance (to choose one title from the many open to misinterpretation), not only in its steps and turns, speaking technically, but in its physically resonant motion to every degree of intensity and rhythm and through its range of experience from light to heavy, bright to dark. Plainly with dance, passive observation is not sufficient to establish a dance culture, but rather active experience in one's own body. We should be able to set dancing people alongside speaking and singing people. Every working person who longs for free movement, in many cases only half-realised at first, should have ·the opportunity for it. The way amateur dance should be encouraged is by means of a new state education which will first discover in this dance the bodily parallel to artistic practice in other fields; amateur dance will become the most important and far-reaching task of a new dance pedagogy responsible both to the art of dance and to the general public.

Amateur dance is always pioneering new ground. Already two avenues of development are clearly distinguishable: social amateur dance in the form of small groups of individuals dancing just for themselves, and the movement choir of larger unified groups. While the first type remains generally restricted to its narrow circle, the movement choir has a festive tendency and this is becoming a promising part of the general aspiration for a new culture in which the festival plays a major part.[1] Everywhere the most progressive youth organisations are seeking to form choirs like these. So it is to be hoped that dance teaching has found in the movement choirs its most widely functioning form, just as music teaching has in the great singing choirs. This should ensure its significant expansion in that it lifts the individual and integrates him into a larger community. So amateur dance should be able to spread in both forms, if . . . indeed if, the great 'but' of any dance education of any dance tradition, if public accountability were not even more inhibiting here than in professional dance. For there is the general uncertainty about the most basic, fundamental principles, the difficulty of notating them, the absence of written works, each a complex of questions, which come together in the concept of a dance script – written dance or dance literacy.

If I wish to give to amateurs the opportunity of meaningful artistic practice, I must be able to give the elements of their material in simple, readily grasped, but not empty or dry form. These elements of our verbal language are collected in our alphabet, indeed somewhat dry and unorganised, but exemplary in usefulness, and also, in tones in the study of music, where they are arranged into fundamental scales. This fundamental material for dance has been discovered and ordered in the movement teaching of Laban. The practical ways in which his ideas are transmitted – often to be found and proven in the successful work with amateurs of various of his pupils – push onwards beyond the personal experience of individual teachers towards comprehensive, readily accessible systemisation. With gifted dance teachers, this means not a tying down of their freedom of method, but rather guidance and support. This (Laban's systemisation) becomes even more necessary when it is no longer the isolated and artistically experimenting pioneers who do this work, but many people as a 'profession'. Such systemisation is inconceivable without movement notation. (Just where such a verbally formalised course and exercise instructions can lead to, one can study as a warning in the widely disseminated countless gymnastics manuals and in their results.)

Good dance teaching of amateur classes will always lead to many play

---

1 Translator's note: *Festkultur* in German.

forms with the studying group; play which is often proved valuable through repetition in rehearsal, and which brings about the development of good motifs, originating from the people and their atmosphere. Only too often and too easily these things get distorted into others, between one class and the next, even in the trained movement memory of the leader. Here one sees in practice, again and again, the need for written records. What if the motif, which carries in it the seeds of compositional form, were first captured in writing, evaluated at leisure and compared and – the best possibility of all – did not need to be worked on in haste and in all the possible disadvantages of the moment, but could be kept for a more favourable time?

Right now the layman is demanding not only unformed play, exercise and improvisation but also, in the progress of his artistic practice, the commitment of the structured work. This gives him an integrated ex-perience, the completed moulded form, the received experience, which, in precision of rehearsal and in the fulfilment of performance in front of a festive gathering of like minds transmits the joy of creation and even more the feeling, the longing, the striving to express everything which has been formed. Just as the social amateur dance is asking for more *ceremonious* and structured dances, so the movement choir is urgently in need of *choral works* of the most varied kind. Its development stands and falls with the possibility of a literature. Works of any length for every occasion must be at the disposal of the movement choir leader if this genre is going to be able to expand.

It would be irresponsible to propagate movement choirs, and encourage people to become movement choir leaders, if the possibility were not there of providing written choral works. I might well say that the circle around Rudolf Laban would not spread the idea of the movement choir so widely without the certainty of this possibility. We do that because we have tested its feasibility in many ways. For years, and in different places, we have studied choral works which have been sent to us in written dance notes; with the development of the Laban script these notes become easier and easier to write and to read, for an ever-increasing number of our associates.

Only with such a notation system is a general extension of amateur dance possible. Imagine if our trusteeship of singing for the world at large were based on the compositional ability of each choir leader. *The written choric and amateur dance work* is the basic requirement, without which one cannot speak of a general dance culture. One can seek strengths from a choir leader's training, in teaching and in leading performances, in bringing people together, in releasing people, but not continuous inventive power, continuous creativity. This situation must lead to drying up, to falseness and worn-out clichés.

The provision of dance literature for amateur dance would, far better than any writing about it, clarify all its questions: its boundaries relative to professional dance, its various forms. It will, one hopes, give it the finest that can be wished for it: a growing series of dances which enable the general public to have experience of what is necessary as regards dance knowledge and dance understanding in works of art.

CHAPTER THREE

Dance Education

Editorial III

Germany had a history of involvement in gymnastic exercise by the general public. *Turnen* (exercise and gymnastics with apparatus) had enjoyed popularity since the early nineteenth century. It developed into a *Körperkultur* movement (physical culture) in which there were a variety of schools. An overview of these is given as background context to the articles on dance education in *Schrifttanz*.

Bess Mensendieck, a Dutch-American, had studied with Geneviève Stebbins, a pupil of Delsarte, and had had medical training. She devised a unique exercise system designed for women's health, based on natural movement patterns, with no extremes of energy output or extension. Good posture, breathing, increased circulation, grace and harmony were the principles upon which the system was based.

The Loheland system developed by Mensendieck through the addition of a spiritual dimension which came through Rudolf Steiner's anthroposophy and, more directly, his wife Marie Steiner's eurhythmy, a system of movement based on the rhythm and physicality of breath and words.

Emil Jaques-Dalcroze's system of eurhythmics, originally an education for musicians through movement, was the most influential system of rhythmic gymnastics. It developed beyond its original purpose into a dance-like method in which music, *plastik* (consideration of the three-dimensional spatial form) and presentation for an audience were all essential ingredients. The Günther School, started in 1923, used an amalgam of the ideals and methods of Mensendieck, Dalcroze and Laban. Dorothée Günther specialised in children's work with her co-operating musician, Carl Orff. By 1930 she had a school-associated performing group, led by Maja Lex.

Rudolf Bode started with Dalcroze but developed his own method with emphasis on the natural rhythms of the body. He called it 'expressive gymnastics'. He had established an influential institute in Munich by 1911.

Additionally there were the Medau and the Loges Schools, Jutta Klamt and Adolf Koch, all teaching varieties of rhythmic exercise.

These formed a context for the profound discussions on movement education in which the dance systems of Wigman, Laban and ballet became influential, both on the level of practice and on philosophic base.

At her school in Dresden, Wigman evolved her vocabulary and her teaching method for both technical training and composition. She developed a progression of work which led to a successful method of professional training, out of which her performing group grew.

In contrast, Laban schools proliferated. The curriculum included training for leadership of amateur dance and movement choirs, as well as for professional dance. All students studied eukinetics, choreutics and 'choreographie'. While Wigman taught her pupils personally, with one or two key assistants, Laban visited his schools as little as once a month. They were directed by his past and present company members and by students who had achieved the Laban Diploma, but not all institutions calling themselves Laban schools were staffed by sufficiently well-trained teachers.

The summer school was a key ingredient of the dance education programmes. Each type of school ran its own course for three to six weeks. For the many Laban schools it was an essential annual meeting place. Here the leading practitioners had the opportunity to work through the principles of their system and their philosophic base.

Nietzsche and Freud were the two men whose revolutionary ideas profoundly disturbed the thinking of artists and teachers at this time. Nietzsche had promoted ecstacy and the Dionysiac, not in preference to Apollonian form but as an essential coexistent to it. Freud had exposed the subconscious and confronted contemporary man with his own innermost secrets. Dorothée Günther voices the anxieties shared by many that the ordinary person may not be able to handle this disequilibrium of the status quo, especially as it manifests itself in the new forms of dance.

She hints also at the friction between the rapturous *Ausdruckstanz* community and the more formal physical culture community who worked towards a healthy and wholesome development of the body and who found ugliness and the grotesque hard to take. But contemporary cabaret artists and many of the new German dancers intentionally presented the darker side of life through themes of death, brutality, greed or lust. The question raised by Günther is whether this intense and all-embracing expressiveness could form a basis for the education of the young person.

She raises the perennial topic of child-centred versus subject-centred teaching and learning. Are we teaching dance or are we teaching people? Laban undoubtedly promoted teaching of the person through dance, the awakening and development of the 'whole' person through confrontation with his or her own movement. Creative expressiveness was essential from day 1 in his method. To the *Körperkultur* teacher such heights were seen as only attainable by the few. But for both schools teaching was a vocation, while for the ballet dancer it was seen by Günther as a job for the unsuccessful performer. Günther also raises the question of the place of amateur dance. Should it be part of the educational system or should it be a recreational activity? This again raises the point: do teaching and learning have to be purely formalised activities?

While Günther is setting forth the issues, Irmgard Thomas takes a stand. Subject teaching is not questioned, neither is indoctrination of movement style, denial of self, nor the relevance or irrelevance of forced beauty in a world in which ugliness is ever present. The idea that ballet itself might develop its vocabulary and methods is not suggested by Thomas.

It is Bronislava Nijinska who deals with the leap of the ballet curriculum into the twentieth century. She has unique expertise in the classical tradition and also in the *avant garde* through her close association with her brother Vaslav. It was Nijinsky who took on the ugliness, the distortion of the body and the asymmetric rhythmic structures of Stravinsky's score in *Sacre du Printemps*. The Dionysiac as propounded by Nietzsche and the erotic as presented by Freud found expression in the work of these two artists. Vaslav's *Jeux* and *L'Après-midi d'un Faune* and Bronislava's *Les Noces* and *Les Biches* are a long way from Irmgard Thomas's 'smiling agony'.

Nijinska's *École du Mouvement* was established in Kiev in 1919. The rationale behind it was to train dancers to be capable of performing in her brother's choreography. This required classically trained dancers who were open to his entirely new aesthetic. Unfortunately her school was short-lived. Her brother's illness caused her to leave Russia and she never established another school where her innovative ideas could be realised.

Nijinska uses the word 'movement' with a particular emphasis. She is used to working in a school in which dance is seen as a series of positions. The motion between the positions has been regarded as less visible, even less important. She is proposing and promoting a new look at the dance material in which the movement itself becomes the all-important feature, the positions being simply something passed through. The word 'movement' means more for her than simple motion. It is a revolutionising influence on the traditional dance material.

The article was originally in Russian. Here it is doubly translated, which exacerbates the problem of trying to understand how she is attempting to express verbally her deep comprehension of the content of movement, essentially a non-verbal domain.

Isadora Duncan had spoken of her dream of seeing the American nation dancing. Here Güldenstein, typical of his period, writes of his vision of a universal dance culture, taking as its model the existing musical culture. The education of dance audiences as well as dance practitioners now becomes the responsibility of dance educators.

To complete this section, we have decided to include an article which did not appear in *Schrifttanz*, but in *Singchor und Tanz* in June 1930. It was, however, discussed in the section for news and notices at the back of *Schrifttanz*. The signatories show the co-operation of the two recently formed dance unions, headed by Laban and Wigman. The syllabus, with its breadth and structure, was pioneering. It was never realised, because of the financial depression followed by the political changes. Today's higher education syllabuses for dance, many of which are remarkably similar to this in content, suggest the foresight which the 1930 plan represented.

VOL. III, NO. 3, NOVEMBER 1930

Why Dance Education?

Dorothée Günther

In its origins modern dance is a breakthrough of self-creative man: man of the twentieth century has become so confident that he can afford to make room for the unconscious. Previous generations were not as confident and therefore afraid to entrust themselves to forces unknown to them; they were bound to fear they could not master these forces. The strong-natured individuals today regard this opportunity as a challenge, and they open doors for themselves which hitherto were closed. Thus they look again at areas which early man felt entirely familiar with, and these come to life. This dawning era which has become so apparent in the entire world of art is called expressionistic. One senses that something is expressed from within man, that is it comes into existence as long as man allows room for these intuitive forces. Thus he reclaimed form as an experience of the soul, colour as a mystical symbol, and dance as a direct spiritual language. Movement has been liberated from its monotonous functional existence. It has developed, as all the other arts, into an expression in its own right instead of merely being a means of expression. These 'movement people' became for us the embodiment of the dancer and we realised that the professional dancer with the particular technique of the old school was inhibited as far as expression was concerned.

Laban, Wigman, Kreutzberg, Palucca, etc. touched us because in their dancing they were expressive, i.e. their movement spoke of what is still seen as basic to life in our nature, but which remains inaccessible to words. One notices that female dancers are more successful in this 'making visible' – perhaps the female organism has not so long a path to reach the forces of the unconscious. Expressionistic dance is in this sense a new language for the human being. Every language arises by creating sounds, repeating them, connecting them, and finally forming them consciously and then teaching them to others; similarly the dancer developed his world of movement forms. And here again man and woman proceed differently: Laban categorising the newly discovered sounds (his swing scales), Wigman entangled in the ecstasy of creating sounds (her first dances, waltzes, etc.). While both are teaching and thus continue on the path begun, Laban evolves the vocabulary and grammar of the new language (his theory of form and his notation), whereas Wigman develops its music (line, rhythm, composition). Their schools pass on the theory of the initiated to enthusiastic students, and the 'dancing nature' in man emerges. It is set free in the 'chosen' and manifests itself in a more or less distorted manner in those who 'felt the vocation'. And here lies the point of attack for the critic, and here is explainable the reluctant attitude of educators of young people. They realise that the aims of dance are different from those of rhythmic gymnastic exercise which emerged during the same period and which is based on a reawakened physicality as a means of giving strength and vitality to man's inner development. The New Dance, on the other hand, produces forces which, unless they are aroused in an 'innocent' body, act to distort and to destroy with just as much strength as they can exert to clarify and to elevate. These are forces indeed of elemental power.

The educator rightly hesitates. His Appollonian world of logically developed educational theory is thus threatened, as Olympia was menaced by the invasion of the Dionysian cult. If we incorporate Dionysus into our world with the same depth of consciousness and the same sense of responsibility, if we give him not only freedom but also restrictions, then he could also be a blessing for us. The dance, as all the other arts, has won its own freedom. Discipline, however, has to be achieved by each dancer individually through his own sense of order and form, for an educational theory of dance does not yet exist, but perhaps is just being born!

An educational theory of dance? The New Dance has created for itself methods for the teaching of the lesson material, but what is still totally absent is its place in the rationale for an education of the human being. Dance will only be able to become of general use when it proves itself to have educational value for young people as well as for adults. We have not reached this state yet, but the dancers themselves strive towards it, as the Munich Dancers' Congress (1930) was able to demonstrate. But to demand is not yet to achieve. And as yet, no dance educators have been trained to prepare professional dancers to become teachers of dance when they cannot find any other sphere of work. Schools to some extent already separate their instruction for dancers and dance educators. However, this is not yet sufficient, for the dance and its teaching methods are still always determined either by the type of the particular dancer who is the founder and director of the school, or by the style of movement, but not by the psychology of individual students or types of students.

The attraction of the student to the master often automatically solves this problem and collects similar types into one school, but within this situation the educational effect of the material is neither tested sufficiently, nor is it used responsibly in the deepest sense. It is too early for criticism, for each art has to find its aims in its own time – but if it wants to shape these aims then it must learn to act educationally. If not, it is reduced to imitation, to circus acts or to grasping for effects, because what attracts a student is more often novelty than depth.

The New Dance has now arrived at *that* stage where ability becomes technique, i.e. it can be learned. Only ten years ago this technique had been newly developed by a few individuals. It became a commercial commodity in the hands of many people, which in too many schools is sold in the name of art. Art does not rescue technique from mechanisation. But educational theory protects art against mechanisation. If we look at the young dance student, we first see the well-trained body, but each person should speak in his own language, therefore the dancer should dance! But when he dances, he dances sadness, pain, the grotesque, joy, a hymn, overwhelmedness, exhaustion, and parody – he seldom dances simply himself, and still more seldom he dances the *dance*. He suffocates in associations, but never in the joy of movement.

It is natural for the mature dancer to associate the dance with the wealth of his emotional life when he composes, that is the process of the creation of a dance work. But how can a young person shape a dance work, if he himself is still a dance novice? He may indeed have often learned his craft astonishingly well, thanks to his young limbs, but nevertheless perceives neither himself nor 'the depth of things'. How does it happen that his uninhibited, young carefreeness does not come across in the dance and delight us by the sheer joy of movement? Why instead does the young dancer attempt a path which is only meant for the gifted few?

The as yet unformed but already practising dance education has methods which urge young people into areas of expression which they do not understand but simply accept. They are led into problems which do not arise for them gradually but which are forced upon them. They are introduced to a form of movement which has grown from the comprehension of problems, but which now is misused. What is certain is that the young person possesses a capacity for feeling far beyond his opportunities for direct experience, and so automatically understands the symbolisation of human emotion. But dance education and expression in dance leading away from revelation rather than towards it is an obscure path to take. Is there a dance school that educates the whole person, the mind as well as the body, one which awakens that which is dormant, orders what is already awake, and prunes the over-exuberant? The majority of schools train the body, transmit material, and push talent and even just-awakening talent into the light. Their sole motivation seems to be the future of the school, forgetting that only talent that has been allowed to develop in its own time can stand firmly on its own feet, whereas one that is just ordinary cannot.

There are the problems of contemporary dance: is modern dance ready for the stage, is it an end in itself, does it have a social function, is it educational material for the young? If we are honest, these problems are central to the training and education of the dancer himself. If he has become deeper and broader through dance education, if he is intellectually more alert, more knowledgeable and more truthful to his own ability, then he will also be more modest and thus more mature, confident and aware. He will risk some experiments of which he is unsure today, but on the other hand he will learn to decline to participate in others in true knowledge of his own ability. Only then do we have the evidence that a dance school is more than a mere filter for talent, which retains some students for the stage or the school's own company. The others, the 'unrecognised' dancers, become teachers of community dance, and thus educators from necessity rather than by vocation. This state of affairs is now unbearable for the dancer, for the enormous opportunities and many strengths of his art are thus left un-exploited. To the outsider this must look like proof that dance, if compared with music, painting, sculpture and poetry, does not stand up to evaluation as an educational means.

Hence we must aim for a dance education which is truly educative.

VOL. III, NO. 2, APRIL 1930

Ballet as Educator

Irmgard Thomas

For years so much has been written on the question of whether ballet is really 'dead' or not; there has been so much discussion about its advantages and disadvantages that I really do not want to add any more to the flood of opinions.

There is only one matter which, till now, has never been appreciated sufficiently, and which I would like to speak about. It concerns the magnificent and unique school of will-power, self-control, and self-denial and the quiet heroism which are all so inseparably connected with ballet. For it is an absolutely false view that ballet is only very demanding in the beginning. On the contrary, at an advanced level, performance has to be improved over and over again, and that means giving one's best in every single exercise. Whoever is capable of that, who comes through it somehow, is a hero, and therefore we should not deny respect to ballet-dancers, even if they do not rise above the average. It is impossible for me to dismiss so much dedication and sincerity, to dismiss such a secure base for further development as artists. Rather, I shall always feel respect for that 'smile', the 'ballet characteristic' which is so frequently criticised, yet behind which lies so much valuable education and good manners. In Asian people, with their ancient culture, this mask is so immensely admired. The ballet-dancer does something quite similar when she glides through the room, standing on pointe. Birdlike she magically creates harmonious movements and smiles at the same time. In the eye of the superficial critic, however, she lacks 'expression'. Occasionally, this might be true, especially so far as dancers of average talent are concerned, but how can one make the art itself responsible for that! When great ballerinas 'smile', the person who sits in the auditorium has received a rich and noble gift. There is no other art in which judgement is made so frequently by only looking at a below-average performance. Yet to achieve even this standard, so much is demanded, and even at the lowest level, a ballet-dancer has to give her best, and they certainly all do! Whatever, indeed, might or might not have been achieved by taking this route, one's life has been enhanced by a unique form of physical training.

The frowned-upon, pale-pink tights, the white tutus, demand a much greater commitment to absolute cleanliness and neatness than do the dark swimming costumes and tunics, which often do not get washed for weeks. I believe I have a right to say that I have met the most well-groomed and nicest women in ballet. Ballet really does 'educate'. The logic of its system creates a more clearly defined personality, the severe discipline strengthens the whole person, and thus bestows a lifelong gift which can never be lost.

One must admit that the former Imperial Russian Ballet, which found its last blossoming in the form of the Diaghilev and Pavlova companies, now unfortunately dispersed, was the elite of the dancing world. They presented a climax unlikely to be reached again in the near future. Their art presented a power, an almost disembodied form of being, which is not based on three or five years of 'training' but on a whole life of total dedication and on daily, exhausting work. If one looks at the faces of the great ballerinas, a unique sister-like characteristic is present in all of them; there are traces of discipline and a very tender expression of self-denial. These people have had to give up everything in order to become what they are, and how significant their achievement is for each one of them. How important it is, affecting one's entire life, to learn to renounce a number of pleasures for the sake of one cause, so that, the following day, one is not tired for the indispensable daily class. It really means placing one's commitment above everything else. This admirable 'ability to endure', and this obsession 'to

54

have control over one's body' even if it cries out with pain, which is often great, is often taken for granted.

When I am in my school, which is attended by many modern dancers and gymnasts, I am frequently astonished at their unbelievable self-pity and intolerance. They can often achieve a great deal, but, apart from a few exceptions, there is one thing they cannot do, that is to serve a cause, willingly, happily, to accept discomfort as a natural accompanying factor. They do not want to sweat; a drop on the forehead is almost regarded as a warning signal that they have worked too hard. They avoid every exercise which might cause pain, and they panic at the thought of developing real dancer's legs. In brief, they would like to have the technique of the 'divine Anna', but without pain, without having to give up anything else, and above all, without calf muscles!

The ideal way of creating a new 'aristocracy of dance' would be to have the kind of large boarding school which the Maryinsky in St Petersburg had in its time. Not only did it train the body but also the spirit and soul, and thus created a dancer who was a complete person. For a ballerina who only has calf muscles is a sad phenomenon, comparable to the poor office worker who has developed a hunched back from constantly sitting down, and whose body is an abnormality of our culture. Generally, our time is still opposed to these ideas. However, a few people have already sensed that the greatly despised old drill does have some good sides to it, and that it might eventually save the situation. For there is no doubt that ballet is not merely concerned with steps, but that it offers opportunities to everyone who feels and who has something to express. In this respect ballet is like every other art, only it is more ennobled by the purest and finest form. Whoever is not capable of appreciating ballet technique, even if it can only be achieved through hard work with many tears, secretly held back at the barre, whoever does not abandon himself to the pure beauty each arabesque strives for, certainly can never be described as an artist. I did not want to praise ballet to the skies, but only wanted to declare my support and to show how much ballet is full of beautiful things which will always remain beautiful.

VOL. III, NO. 1, APRIL 1930

On Movement and the School of Movement

Bronislava Nijinska

Movement is the principal element in dance, its plot. A modern school of choreography must introduce movement into dance technique, it must provide a basis for the theory and the mechanics of dance.

Colour – is the material of painting.

Sound – the material of music.

Movement – the material of dance.

Movement gives to dance a life of its own. Only movement can stimulate an audience.

Rhythm lives only in movement. Movement makes the body active.

In the plot, movement must be uninterrupted – otherwise the life of the plot is interrupted. The moment that movement is taken away from the body, away from the artist's intention, an endless interruption starts, by no means the same as a pause, because a pause is also a movement in the plot, similar to breathing.

In the transition from one position to another, upon the change of one position into the other, the body should not only alter its place. In choreography the change of place must be movement. In the theatre the artist's body must not only walk up and down but must simultaneously act (i.e. forward the plot).

Each machine, made for a particular purpose, has a certain predetermined movement; it has its own form – it is the result of a mechanism assembled together.

The form, the three-dimensional form (*Plastik*), the position of the body, must arrive as the result of movement.

Choreographic movement must possess its own organic force (which is different for each composition). Its breath, its rhythm, its life, must take on a spatial form.

No motion can be inserted into a thought-up, static, lifeless form; any choreographic composer, and creator of a choreographic work, must know this above all.

The choreographer has to make the movement comprehensible to the performing artist, he must instruct the artist as to how a movement assumes a form which is visible to the audience.

So this is the purpose of the present-day modern choreographic school, the 'School of Movement' . . .

The words *Plastik, Geste,* in their theatrical sense, are no longer used; these words have been replaced, by many, by the term movement.

But one should question this:, does one really provide movement instead of *Geste, Plastik* and *Pose,* or is it only a terminological renaming?

In the choreographic art, scarcely anyone, until now, has really perceived movement clearly (perhaps has simply not been conscious of it). Seldom has anyone performed a dance and 'signed' it with movement; seldom does anyone 'sing' the movement of his dance, and I scarcely believe that the audience 'hears' the melody of the movement with their eyes, that they see the form of this movement of the dancer.

The artist, especially the choreographic artist, must totally command movement, see and recognise the content of movement – he must help himself to find the movement as the material of his art.

The stage artist aims for 'grace', 'elegance', the appearance of an 'athletic pose'; he perceives this in the positions of the body, of groups, contrived or provided for him by the choreographer, in 'pictorial poses'.

The dancer, in dance technique exercises, aims to accustom the body to a series of 'positions' (which is quite unavoidable, since the positions are the basis on which movement is maintained); but unfortunately the whole of the dancer's attention is frequently concentrated only on the comprehension of these poses or positions.

1. The position – the body is in a certain form; the proportion of the distances between arms, torso and legs is fixed.
2. The position – the start and finish of the movement; the station through which the movement passes. The main point on which the portrayal of the movement is based.
3. All movements are concentrated on the positions. The positions provide the shape for the body, in which the movement is made known.
4. The position leads the body, out of one plane into the others, it prepares the body for a certain movement, it helps each movement to be performed freely.
5. The position provides a balance, a harmony between the movement and the body shape; it gives balance to the body and shape to the movement.[1]

The dancer who, when transferring from one position into another, takes trouble to step into a well-rehearsed position, restricts his dance action to a series of poses through a lifeless space, his dance remains unconscious between these positions; he does not connect the latter by the life of the movement.

The 'classical school' of dance long ago found the principal movements, *pas,* the steps from which the dance is built up; but the life of these *pas* movements is decided on purely mechanical criteria, solely through the metrical factors and through the beat of the music; but it does not make the transition into another rhythmic-melodic form.

Neither the rhythm, nor the variety, of musical works, nor the variety of epochs of music and of action, bring about an alteration of the technical *pas.* They are always performed in the same way, according to the established manner, which is easy for the dancer once studied.

The school of classical dance studies, as movements, only particular *pas,* but the secret of providing something between the positions remains alien to the ballet-masters and also to dancers.

1 From *The School of Movement* (Theory of Choreography) by Bronislava Nijinska, Kiev, 1920. This is a footnote in the original article.

The great dancers, such as Vaslav Nijinsky and Anna Pavlova, uplifted us by their dances, because within them a true inner nature of movement proclaimed itself. (Of course, this happened unconsciously, through their genius, not their schooling.)

It is notable that these two artists, creators of a whole epoch of dance art, aroused an unheard-of interest in dance throughout the whole world and yet they have not found any real successors.

Some people saw in them something unearthly, others expressionist art, *Plastik,* separated from the old classical form, but no one saw the true technique of movement.

Already many legends have been made up about Vaslav Nijinsky which, however, do not enable the young listener to visualise Nijinsky's dance in any way, or at least not fully; but no one is working on the perpetuation of his complete dance style, that is, these elements brought about by the movement which are entirely unique to him and from which Nijinsky's brilliant dance style was composed.

The last 25 years brought with them a revolution in the choreographic art, but only in choreographic stage works. Schools have learnt nothing from it.

Nor has the world ever seen such a quantity of dance schools of all kinds, all however restricted to 'friends' or 'enemies' of the classical school.

The former want to retain the old 'classical' school entirely intact, the latter deny everything in it and want to found an entirely new school.

Here undoubtedly the reformers are wrong. Their idea of a better understanding of dance through the search for a new school is confused with the basic theory of dance mechanics.

The classical school simply is the foundation of dance.

Every reformer presents us with a gift, but at the same time robs us of the inventions made by the genius of former masters of the art of dance.

One must proceed with the greatest care, with the greatest precision in the development of new ideas, if these should cause the destruction of the bases of the existing school systems.

One must totally sweep away useless things, but one must not disregard, or even destroy, the things that constitute the foundation, the basis of the mechanics of the art of dance.

This must become the principal duty of the dance reformers, just as they must introduce into the schools the new 'inventions' of the creative artists of our time. Only then shall we have the possibility, without demolishing the old, of providing for our 'new' artistic life from its traditions.

To the extent that the present-day choreography has distanced itself from ballets in a purely classical mode, the present-day school must be more complete and possess greater dance technique.

If we compare the compositions of the older ballet-masters with the present-day school of ballet, then we note in it an image of the structure of the dances. All *pas* movements of the classical ballet are included in this school and support the ideal performance of the work of art, providing the necessary elements of the dance technique. Male and female dancers of the present day use all the material contained in such compositions, the actual movements, in their daily practice (in the exercises of the technique class). *Pirouettes, battus, fouettés,* all these are material for the compositions. The inspired 'inventions' of a master of dance, everything provided by the choreographer, all the *pas,* have their basis and their realisation in the classroom.

But nowadays we see that some schools study only the old dance technique, and the others, in contrast, deny the existing fundamentals of dance mechanics – and seek to discover these very things anew!

Don't we surely arrive at the view that present-day dance schools are degenerate, that they are not capable of keeping pace with present-day art and providing anything new?

These schools do not give the artist a sufficient education for him to be able to work with an innovative choreographer. The Russian Ballet has not concerned itself with the idea of creating its own school. Normally, artists of this company were traditionally trained and came from a variety of teachers and theatres.

Often what is considered as the individuality of a performer is only weakness and choreographic ignorance. Such an artist, in the performance of the composition presented to him, sees and provides only what is within his ability. Such dancers reproduce the choreographic score in a fundamentally wrong way, killing the individuality of the work. The actual composition of the choreographer is destroyed, without being given the 'true idea', the power, the rhythm of the melody, which the author wanted to express. The dancer is unable to bring anything of it about, not necessarily by an absence of talent, but because of inadequate training.

But what is the choreographer to do with all these new ideas, if the earlier path to art through training is denied to the interpreting artist, if he has not studied it, if he lacks the necessary technique and mechanics? The choreographer can only give himself the task of correctly teaching all the *pas* to the artists, for he has no further possibilities.

Such a work does not receive a new nature, a new life. One can observe this today when even the most famous dancers appear in new works. If the choreographer requires a new dance movement, one which is mechanically very difficult, then although the artist will manage to glide over easily from one of these *pas* into another, the nature (quality) of the dance movement will not correspond at all with the modern choreographic technique. Such a dance is like the uniform seam made by a sewing machine, there is no life in the movement.

Everything appears aimless to us, if the body of the artist only moves in order to assume one or another position or pose, however new and interesting these may be. However expressively this choreographic form may be thought out, it is not able to stir us if it is not provided through the movement, if the movement is not inherent in the form.

However deftly, and like the 'movies', the body of the dancer changes its positions, it is nevertheless not the choreographic movement which we have been discussing here, but only an aimless, meaningless change of shape, an overcoming of mechanical difficulties.

The performing artist must provide dance through movement; he must include movement in the same way that he includes life, in the plastic form of the dance. He must pour out the melody of the dance through his body, for the audience can only comprehend the movement.

Not every note (sound) is music, not every movement is choreography.

You must make the technique of the movement powerful, in order to create choreographic works.

You must master proficiency in movement, in order to be able to express your art.

VOL. III, NO. 2, JUNE 1930

Foundations for a Dance Culture

Gustav Güldenstein

> Wär' nicht das Auge sonnenhaft,
> Die Sonne könnt' es nie erblicken;
> Läg' nicht in uns des Gottes Kraft,
> Wie könnt' uns Göttliches entzücken?
> (Goethe)

> Were not the eye full of the sun,
> It never could catch glimpses of its light;
> If God's own power were not in us,
> How could a heavenly thing bring us delight?

If someone is drifting in a current, what will he do? Swim – swim! He will hardly meditate on the meaning of swimming or his style of movement.

This analogy might throw some light on the situation in which teachers of dance, gymnastic exercise, rhythm etc. find themselves. They have to fight a constant battle for survival which demands that they always have to attract new students. The problems resulting from this rivalry are such that they hardly have a chance to contemplate whether they really should be teaching dance, exercise or similar activities, nor do they have time to think about the 'style' of their teaching. Superficial successes alone often determine all their actions. If we stay with our original analogy we might say that they are swimming as hard as they can and they only have one aim: to reach dry land.

In view of this situation we should give the questions of 'why' and 'how' some serious thought. For all those who can think beyond their own welfare there exists a moral obligation to examine the purpose of their actions from a less subjective angle. Furthermore such an investigation might even have practical advantages; for, in the long run, it is only the teacher who fully believes in his work and can see it in the appropriate context, who will have genuine success. Let us start by asking ourselves: what is to become of all those students who are taking classes in dance, exercise, rhythmic gymnastics and whatever we want to name all these activities which essentially all strive for the same aims? Only a very small number of students will become true artists. A much greater proportion will join the teaching profession; and the number of these future teachers will be augmented by those who in the beginning had dreamt of an artistic career, but then realised that requirements were higher than they had thought originally. Most of the students, however, are amateurs, who attend exercise or dance classes for various reasons, ranging from genuine enthusiasm to motives such as 'I want to lose a few pounds' or 'my friend Emma takes lessons, too'. If we are serious about justifying our existence as dance educators, such students (who only attend for these reasons) should not merely be seen as welcome customers who keep our business profitable. Let us use the term 'dance exercise' for all those activities which are concerned with the teaching of amateurs and of which the more or less clearly stated aim is to increase general artistic ability through physical activity. What we have to ask ourselves is: 'What can dance exercise offer towards the foundation of a dance culture?'

We thus consciously ignore a number of questions, first of all the question whether a dance culture is really desirable. If we pose such a question, then we have to admit that it is inseparable from the wider issue of whether an artistic culture *per se* is a valuable ideal for mankind. Furthermore, we leave out the decisive significance of the creative artist for a dance culture. Neither do we discuss methods, and we emphasise the factors that unite a dance culture rather than those that lead to disharmony. Many other questions need to be left unanswered if we want to keep our original question in clear focus.

Let us use existing musical culture as a model. (I am aware of the fact that dancers do not like this constant comparison of dance and music. It is understandable that nobody likes to be constantly reminded of the example set by an elder sibling. Nevertheless, we should concede that, in our present-day culture, music is the elder sister from whom the younger one can learn a great deal.)

Therefore, how does music education promote a musical culture?

1. It tries to make the layman receptive to the work of art.
2. It tries to inspire and develop his own creativity.
3. It wants to transmit technical skills appropriate to his abilities and ambitions (instruments, voice and composition).
4. Finally it wants to awaken his analytical awareness of music: an understanding of structure, of history etc.

We must ask the question: what is to become of the layman educated in this manner? It is because of his good and comprehensive education that the music-lover will not mistake himself for a professional artist. He might perform for his family and friends and he can fully enjoy his own successes in composition. But it is due to his good education that he is not a 'dilettante' in the negative sense of the word; he will form the nucleus of a truly good and appreciative audience.

Now, what about the teachers for a dance culture? What do they need to consider?

1. Appreciation of the work of art. How do we experience dance as a work of art? Through the eye and through physical response. Therefore we need to develop these two senses. The student whose receptiveness possesses a certain maturity should be able to see a movement sequence in his mind as well as feeling it in his body, and then to reproduce either graphically or physically.
2. His own creativity is awakened during improvisation and composition classes.
3. An amateur's technique will always remain limited, nevertheless it needs to be clean and based on correct principles. One of the amateur's tasks will be to reproduce the creations of others. This is part of 'technique', as it presupposes a certain technical maturity. It is also relevant to our first objective, as we can only be fully open to something if we have at one time been actively involved in it. Here dance notation can serve as an important educational tool.
4. An analytical awareness of dance is the best tool an amateur can have in order to distinguish between self-indulgence and a genuine work of art.

If we agree that only dance students who have been educated in such a manner can form a truly appreciative audience for dance, and that no genuine dance culture can exist without such an audience, we can thereby reassure all teachers of 'dance exercise'; far from there being too many teachers of dance, there are far too few. We could do with thousands more, before we even approach a dance culture comparable to our existing musical culture. But it all depends on the teachers who constantly have to make greater demands, first of themselves and then of their students. It is only in the rarest cases that the teacher himself is a creative artist, but he must always remain in lively contact with the art itself. If teachers restrict themselves to technique and lifeless formulae, they might create a 'dance fashion' but never a 'dance culture'.

FROM *SINGCHOR UND TANZ*, YEAR 47, NO. 12, 15 JUNE 1930

Plans for Dance in Higher Education

Joint proposal by the Deutscher Tänzerbund and the Deutsche Tanzgemeinschaft[1]

Aims

Critics and the general public have been unanimous in their decision to acknowledge the new artistic dance in Germany as an essential cultural asset. In order to achieve equality with music and the visual arts, dance needs to be taught at college level – something dancers have been striving for for decades.

This new college has to be a central institution specialising in dance as a performance art and in movement study, as well as offering training courses for teachers intending to work with either professional or amateur dancers. The main function of this college is to provide a course for advanced students which enables them to study dance, dance education and choreography at degree level.

Rationale

It is essential to find a common concept in the form of higher education for the different forms of dance training which nowadays take place in the various private schools and stage schools. This unification as well as a form of advanced study are necessary in order to develop the quality of performance and the intellectual capacity of our dancers to a maximum level. It is only then that dance can become a completely independent form of art and that it can be recognised as the basis of all theatrical creation.

This aim can only be achieved if the college produces people who are capable of being leaders in the professional world of dance performance and choreography.

It is also important that the training of teachers conforms to an equally

1 Both these organisations were dancers' unions.

high standard, as they will be responsible for the education of the next generation of dancers.

In this sense, the college will create a lively tradition which is constantly developing and which will contribute to a more unified style of dance.

In order to maximise the social values of dance, we also have to include the promotion and the support of amateur dance in our college programme. Otherwise there is a real danger that the constantly growing amateur movement, which is so valuable in creating a new form of folk art, will be exposed to poor teaching and to a lack of direction. To avoid this, the College of Dance would become a central place of advice and direction for the dance education of children and adults.

In order to do justice to such a variety of tasks, the College of Dance would not only be a teaching institute, but also a place for research in the field of movement study.

The Organisation

Essentially the College of Dance is divided into practical and theoretical areas.

Theoretical as well as practical fields of study are divided into core subjects and optional subjects. Theory is taught in the same manner as it is taught in universities, i.e. by lectures and seminars.

Practical subjects are taught in classes. The classes are leading up to master classes which, in the same way as in other art schools, are taught by important contemporary dance artists.

This system will give the students a character-forming influence and it will also ensure the development of a strong tradition.

In order to prepare the students for the various dance professions, the school has to work out a special syllabus which contains obligatory and optional subjects.

The following syllabus does not yet specialise according to the various professional directions, but it gives an overview of all the subjects to be taught at the College of Dance.

SUBJECT AREAS

Practical

I *Core Subjects*
   1. Dance as a form of art:
      (a) technique and composition (technique, increase and enrichment of expression in dance, inspiration and promotion of own compositions)

    (b) mime

    (c) dance in the theatre (opera and drama)

  2. Teachers' training for teaching professional students:

    (a) direction for solo dance

    (b) direction for group dance

    (c) lesson and syllabus planning

    (d) 'directing' of movement

  3. Teachers' training for teaching amateurs:

    (a) *Reigen*

    (b) movement choirs

    (c) lesson planning

II *Optional Subjects*

  1. Music for the dancer (musicality, rhythm, piano, composition)

  2. Theatre management (costume, make-up, lighting, technical apparatus, stage design)

  3. Ballet

  4. Folk dance, 'exotic dance', social dance

Theory

I *Core Subjects*

  1. Movement study (general movement study, theory of harmony, theory of composition)

  2. Dance education

  3. Notation

  4. Dance history

II *Optional Subjects*

  1. Psycho-physiology

  2. Musical theory

  3. Kinesiology

  4. Sociology of dance

Teaching Materials

Lessons must make use of all modern teaching materials, especially a comprehensive library and an archive, which must also contain films, records, sheet music and notated dances.

Faculty and Management

Eight full-time and four part-time staff, some teaching more than one subject. All posts of responsibility are determined by vote from within the College staff (e.g. the director and the co-director).

  Guest teachers are invited when needed.

Students
1. Full-time students
2. Students from other colleges who want to specialise in one area of dance and only study that one particular subject
3. Visiting students (e.g. only for particular lectures)

Entry Requirements
Only students who have completed three years of study in a private school and have passed the examination of that school, are admitted to the entry examination.

Length of Study
At least two years which finish with an examination in order to obtain a diploma (equivalent to a degree).

Entitlements
The diploma entitles to admission to the following professions:
1. Solo dancer
2. Choreographer and director
3. Teacher for professionals and amateurs
4. Independent director of a school (only after a one-year teaching practice)

Finance
The same as for other art colleges and universities.[2]

Signed by: 1. Tänzerbund
R. V. Laban
Enger Friedebach
Olga Brandt-Knack
Lizzie Maudrick
Martin Gleisner

2. Tanzgemeinschaft
Mary Wigman
F. Emmel
Ernst Ferand
Gret Palucca
Margarete Wallmann

---

2 That is, by the State (editors).

CHAPTER FOUR

Dance and its Supportive Arts

Editorial IV

The first three decades of the twentieth century saw a variety of innovative approaches which explored possibilities in the relation of dance and sound. In the Dalcroze School this relationship was one of total dependence. Dalcroze's use of movement to educate musicians led to dancers following the musical beats slavishly and using arm movements which corresponded with the musical phrasing. Although Isadora Duncan stated her dependence on music for emotional inspiration, her dances were not tied to the structure of the music. She also challenged the notion that the music of such composers as Beethoven and Gluck was unsuitable for dance.

In the ballet world Diaghilev's artists sought to establish perfect harmony and equality between the different media. Soviet ballet took a step hitherto unprecedented in the ballet world: traditional music was replaced by noise bands and the recitation of poetry. The developing modern dance in the USA, too, experimented. Ruth St Denis established her music visualisation theory and practice, and later Helen Tamiris and Doris Humphrey tried to free the dance altogether from music by dancing in silence. Dances without music were also performed by Laban and Wigman in Germany. In his attempt towards achieving the autonomy of dance, Laban explored the organic rhythm of the body and the sound of motion, step, word and breath which come from the dancer himself.

This revolution, begun in Munich and Ascona in the 1910s, was at an interesting stage by the time *Schrifttanz* was first published. Dancers had as their associates musicians of a high calibre: men who were composers, percussionists, pianists and conductors, and also musicologists and critics. The manifold and complex ways in which motion and sound might relate, once the autonomous nature of each had been acknowledged, was being explored. The importance of sound and silence, motion and stillness is evident but the concept of total independence, the coexistence without corelationship of sound and motion, well-known to dance now through the work of John Cage and Merce Cunningham, had not yet arrived.

Live music was the only option for performances, usually under the control of a pianist or a conductor of an instrumental group. Collaboration of choreographer and composer was an everyday actuality.

Dancers had to be musically educated, and musically literate. First-rank dancers worked with first-rank musicians, many having long associations. Wagner-Régeny worked with Laban, as did Friedrich Wilckens, who then joined for a lifelong partnership with Harald Kreutzberg. Jooss's co-operating musician was Fritz Cohen, Wigman's were Will Goetze and Hanns Hasting and Günther's was Carl Orff. Ernst Krenek, whose sensational jazz opera *Jonny spielt auf* was first performed in 1927, wrote for Laban's Vienna Festzug.

Alfred Schlee tackles the very real problems encountered daily from a musician's point of view in his article. As a music publisher he had an interest and an expertise which he used to look deeply at the difficulties for the musicians who played for and with dancers. The last part of his article gives us an insight into the very beginnings of recorded music for dance, but at a time when each recording was specially made, involving close co-operation between the dancer and the conductor.

Hanns Hasting, Mary Wigman's accompanist, tackles the relationship of musical harmony and dance as they both affect space through the listener/spectator's response. The reader will recognise his description of movements which are 'effective in creating space' as similar to the art philosopher Susanne Langer's concept of the virtual images created in artworks. The movement stops at the body's extremities but its effect enlivens the space around the dancer, penetrating it with energy and focus. The atonality of Schoenberg's new approach to harmony was well known to Mary Wigman, originally through her association with Laban, whose space harmony concepts related analogously to Schoenberg's. At Monte Verità and in Zurich at the Dada gatherings Schoenberg's innovative compositions were played. What Hasting does not include is that movement too has basic harmonic laws, clustered around the verticality of gravity. There is a need for off-balance and flight to return to the stability of the vertical of a grounded stance, reminiscent of the need for resolution of musical tensions into the groundedness of 'doh'; that is, back to the base note of the key around which the melody is written.

Hans Redlich, having studied with Carl Orff, was in a strong position to pursue Orff's musical innovations in the Günther School. His article presumes some knowledge of Orff's methods of sound making. Not only percussion but also body sounds were used, with vocal rhythmicising on nonsense words as well as guttural sounds, claps and snapping fingers. The term *Gebrauchsmusik* is translated as 'utility music', which is not an entirely satisfactory English equivalent. It is a term first coined by Hindemith for a special kind of music for use with amateurs, sometimes for special occasions but also simply for use at home or in school. Carl Orff was especially associated with *Gebrauchsmusik* and so too was Kurt Weill, his contemporary, whose successful and approachable *Threepenny Opera* was premièred in 1928. The similarity of concern in dance and music for specific kinds of work for amateurs is typical of this period of German culture.

The article by Charlotte Rudolph is the first one known on dance photography and gives some insight into the state of photography at that time. It reflects the state of understanding of motion *vis-à-vis* position in dance practice.

Alfred Brasch's article reveals how ambivalent was the grasp of many dancers as well as many dance critics of the latter's role; and how difficult it was, and indeed still is, to get away from the voyeur approach of some critical writers. André Levinson, a balletomane; Joseph Lewitan, editor of the monthly magazine *Der Tanz;* John Schikowski, a historian; and Hans Brandenburg, the art critic and writer, were the dominant critics in *Schrifttanz's* time.

VOL. II, NO. 1, JANUARY 1929

Problems in the Relationship between Music and Dance

Alfred Schlee

Dance is entering a new era. After ten years of revolutionary fluctuations in thought, ever-changing initiatives, and the most violent arguments, we now stand at the beginning of a definite conceptual clarification. Dance notation presents us with the means to embark on the construction of a dance theory of harmony and form, and to direct precise research into the manifold ways in which bodily expression and spatial patterning interact.

The situation compels us to clarify the relationship of dance to its supportive arts, and the connections between dance and music deserve our primary consideration. Quite enough has been written about the problem. But the result of the theoretical considerations and practical experiments so far undertaken can only have a short validity. The dancer who is oriented to bodily expressiveness demands that the music has total subordination, and adapts itself to the unfolding expression of his dance. An artistic statement primarily based on expressiveness forces formal construction into the background, and requires oneness in all its components. A contrapuntal combination between dance and the formal elements of the music is excluded, so long as expression is the predominant artistic element in the dance. Hence also in the music the formal elements have to take second place to the expressive ones. Thus expressionist dance led to an excessive emphasis on interpretation, which became the connecting link between dance and music. In practice, the greatest problems must arise from the improvisatory character of this connection. Almost all efforts that offered a solution which was to some extent satisfactory for the dancer were compromises. The music often had to be distorted in performance, sometimes contorted out of all recognition, in order to follow the dancer. As a real consequence, people attempted dance without music, which nevertheless was not satisfactory. Gradually there came into existence an orchestra for dance, whose make-up largely corresponded to the needs of the dancer.

There were few instruments: piano and percussion, sometimes solo wind players. The percussion developed in use and treatment a really virtuoso sophistication, which related mainly more to the tone colour than to the rhythmical element. This orchestra for dance brought about a wealth of dance activity and met the main requirement of the dancer: it could very largely suit him. An important feature: dancers, not musicians, play the most important instruments. Even on the piano there is a player with strongly visual empathy. The orchestra keeps track of the dancer visually, following his movements down to the finest detail and ready at every moment to get closer to him through improvisation. Sometimes there was an absolutely astonishing amalgam of dance and music.

However tempting this kind of accompaniment for dance may appear to be at first for the dancer, its limits are still too narrowly drawn. Its effect is directed too much at the dancer, and too little at the spectator-listener. The limitation of the orchestra produces monotony and one can detect all too clearly that this orchestra for dance has been created, not by inner necessity, but primarily by extrinsic problems. As dance submitted itself to the theatre, the question of music for dance came to a crisis, the dangers of which could be avoided simply by the transformation of the new dance theatre.

When the overemphasis on expression in dance gives way to a spatial-formal construction, music also attains another position within the frame-work of the dance work of art. The link is now produced no longer by the synchronisation of expressive tension and release, but by correspondence of rhythmical structure and formal construction in music and in dance. Thus in place of the subjective elements of feeling there come facts of the matter which can be established on both sides in writing. This fresh orientation naturally alters also the composition of music for dance. What is preferred is music with a clear structure, with sustained rhythmic phrases and without dramatic pathos. The music gains in independence, and no longer has to be constructed slavishly on rhythm and dynamics that are solely derived from the body. The contrapuntal treatment of musical and dance forms releases the music from the task of being merely a background. Of course the ear must not be overloaded by music that is too demanding. Since experience shows that simultaneous and equal receptiveness of eye and ear is impossible, care must be taken that the musical impression does not disturb the visual one.

Now the musical interpretation assumes a totally different significance in the association of dance with music. In expressionist dance, the interpretation was more important than the work to be performed. In contrast, in dance which is formally constructed, the interpretation loses its individual significance. Once the desired rendering of the music has been settled, then the interpretation must derive totally from the work itself and only have the aim of repeating this particular rendering with the greatest possible precision in exactly the same way at each performance. This gives rise to fresh difficulties for the accompanist of dance. Whereas it was previously impossible to follow the expressive fluctuations of the dancer when using a larger orchestra, now it is almost unattainable for the conductor to cut out his own intuitive artistic impulse. Despite the greatest efforts by the conductor, variations will occur again and again, which are an immense handicap to the dancer. For he can only give his concentration to his dance, only be wrapped up in the creation of his own life of shapes, if the flow of the music proceeds absolutely reliably and without variation. During performance, the dancer cannot communicate to the conductor any individual variations in interpretation. The dancer does not even have the opportunity to protect himself against a wrong tempo set up by the conductor. It is simply given to him and far too often what happens is that the effectiveness of the dance is not only inhibited, but is virtually destroyed, if the dancer has to direct his attention consciously to the orchestra. It is only the release from this non-artistic distraction that can lead him to the full development of his whole personal effective power.

The objective of the dancer must thus be to exclude an interpreter, who is inevitably dependent on the human feelings of the moment, and to seek a musical accompaniment in which the performance cannot be altered by any external influence. This requirement leads to the attempt to use a mechanical instrument for dance accompaniment.

A mechanical instrument keeps one interpretation that has been given to it, and makes repetition possible as often as desired, with exact precision. The mechanical piano and organ have already reached such a technical perfection that there cannot be any doubts about their use. But even the gramophone and film, as instruments for reproduction of orchestral music, will doubtless themselves be able to replace an orchestra in the widest sphere in the foreseeable future.

Indeed in a small way the gramophone has already found an entry into the world of the professional dancer. It has proved itself in its introduction in the studio for class work. It would be even more widely introduced into teaching, if there were a collection of discs available which took account of the dancer's requirements.

The mechanical instrument is even used already for artistic work. Schlemmer put on the *Triadic Ballet* and Yvonne Georgi *The Strange House* with Hindemith's mechanical organ. In Essen a Honegger orchestral ballet was rehearsed with a setting for electric piano, made specially for it. The experiences arising from these experiments are to be discussed in the next issue.

In the choreographic work itself, nothing would alter. The use of the mechanical instrument even at the rehearsal stage will provide the dancer with a tremendously exact familiarity with the music, and will allow him to create an even closer compositional connection between the dance and the music. All the innumerable contingencies, which at present threaten the dancer because of the orchestra, the surprises which come with the first orchestral rehearsal, disappear. In contrast, each musical nuance can be considered and attended to from the very beginning of the work on the dancing.

The number of mechanical pieces of music already in existence, which can be considered for dance, is still very limited, but this lack can be filled easily and quickly. Only the choice of the piece of music might be made more difficult in that no alteration can be made to the musical performance once recorded, even before the start of the work on the dancing.

A solution free from compromise can be found if the individual dance companies themselves have the rolls, discs or films made for their works. Then the artistic director has the opportunity of settling every detail there with the musicians. If one is dealing with an existing work, the interpretation can take account of the basic requirements of the dance. If the music is newly-composed, then the factor of 'interpretation' can actually be almost totally excluded. Practical collaboration between the composer and the engineer during orchestral recording will generate a series of absolutely new sound effects, which can only be achieved by means of a mechanical instrument. One example is the increased prominence of solo instruments, an effect which one could call musical enlargement and which enables the solo instrument to predominate over the accompanying instruments to an extent and power that is never possible in the concert hall. Such examples can be extended at will. Reference can be made to those opportunities for effects which at present are further in the future, which can result from a collaboration of dance and sound film. Here, practical experiments directly in the area of music for the dancer will create a wealth of new stimuli and opportunities for collaborative possibilities.

VOL. IV, NO. 2, OCTOBER 1931

Sound and Space

Hanns Hasting

The relationship of dance and music in respect of their common mode of development has its most important premise in the relationship of its elements. To the degree that the basic expressions of human feeling are capable of fusing with one another so that their basic identity can no longer be distinguished, the work of art in its crystallisation will show a unitary character. We had recognised the relationship of dance and music as resting on the relationship of the elements: rhythm to rhythm / gesture to melody / space to sound.

In what follows I isolate the elements of space on the one hand, and of sound on the other, from the total structure. I do so with the knowledge that these very two elements, being least accessible to direct experience, need special investigation.

Everyone can sing a melody, everyone can make a gesture, there is some sense of rhythm in every dancer and in every musician. Of all the elements it is space and sound, suitably used, which are not only the outpouring of elemental human feeling but also bring man's artistic intellect to the fore. Sensing space, creating space, filling space, whatever one wishes to call it from the dancer's point of view, sensing sound, creating sound from the musician's point of view, are indeed above all other elements of composition and as such need a greater detachment from the subjective.

Composition literally means: putting together. A gesture or a melody cannot be 'put together'. They are 'intuitively invented'. Paths in space and complexes of sound are 'put together' indeed on the basis of the 'invented' motif, but without eliminating the use of the intellect. This is how it is.

Paul Bekker regards the arrival of harmony as a time when a foreign element entered music. He calls harmony: 'space-creating' and 'giving a sense of spaciousness'. Let us accept this as 'harmony'. In what follows we have to investigate how far, and especially whether at all, musical harmony that is creating space has a valid relationship to dance that is creating space.

Without searching too far, what should we understand by space-creating harmony? It is an expression of human response to sound, which logically can never escape intellectual verification. A series of three sounds, initially the subjective expression of the composer, is totally accessible to intellectual analysis. On this duality of subjectivity and objectivity there rests the whole of western musical response, based as it is especially on harmony. Seen from this point of view, harmony producing the effect of space reveals itself not as an expression that is predominantly intuitive, as one could have supposed instinctively on the basis of primary musical experience, but as a thoroughly rational, defined expression. Inasmuch as a harmonic movement relates again and again to the cadence as a formula, the spatial experience created by it will not be fluid, unreal, intangible, but will be stable, grounded, real.

It is not like that with dance. Even though the dancer, like no other artist, always has to deal with space as a reality, not nearly enough attention is paid to it, to composition within a reasonable space frame. On the contrary, space for dance, the experience of space in dance, grows from beyond the limitations of dance's physicality and from the real limits of the space into a virtually created space and a response to space, which resist every attempt to measure them. It is up to the receptive spectator how far he is capable of responding to a gesture, the effect of which extends beyond the measurable space. On the other hand it is up to the dancer how far he is capable of creating 'space' and getting it to have an effect. But the fact is that space in dance is not one constant, definite entity, but is a fluid, intangible, imaginary thing.

From this recognition we must observe that the word harmony, meaning having an effect in space (in music), is not a valid expression for dance which has an effect in space, and a connection is not possible on such a premise. We have to regard 'harmony' as an expression of human response to sound. And it is just this side of music that has experienced the most severe change in the last century. Harmony, in the sense of the relationship of one sound with another, has been eradicated as an integral component of musical composition, and 'functionless sound' has been put in its place. The governing of the relationship of sounds by laws has ceased to exist, and the enquiring listener finds no objective point of reference. The spatial effect of sound which comes from this new response to sound has a totally other aspect. The objective lack of interrelationship of the sounds, the un-groundedness and unreality of the 'putting together' emphasises the limited nature of the harmonic effect in space and provides the inconstant, unreal space.

As can now easily be seen, this new response to sound provides the appropriate link to dance, and dance gives renewed evidence of fruitful influence on musical composition. As we have already seen earlier, dance demands an organic mode of development from a piece of music which is suitable for it, and now as part of this it demands a new response to sound, and it is these simultaneous inner demands that are a musical mode of composition purely of our time. Space, as an element of dance construction on the one hand, and absolute sound as an element of musical construction on the other, both aim at the creation of an imaginary, unreal response to space. They find their obvious and ideal fusion in a dance-music work of art.

VOL. IV, NO. 2, OCTOBER 1931

The Function of Music in the Context of the Günther School

Hans F. Redlich

The present-day musical and critical discussion likes to emphasise the demand for purposefulness in its art, and is always endeavouring, with increasing urgency, to legitimise, in a sociological, political and aesthetic way, the present aims of music. Music has moved away from the concerns of the ordinary person, back to practical 'playing areas'. Because of this, I, as a musician who has become thoughtful, feel drawn to make an explicit reference to an organisation working at the present time, in which music is assigned a role that is thoroughly independent, indigenous and 'usable'. By this I refer to the School for Gymnastics, Rhythmics, Music and Dance in Munich, founded and directed by Dorothée Günther. The main contribution of this School is to have done away with the old concept 'music for dance', as being an arbitrary musical episode, which was involved to a certain extent in the content-related associations of gestures and sound. Simultaneously the school has newly questioned the interpretability of musical content by gesture and rhythm. I realise that other dance/pedagogic pioneers have also taken part in this contribution, and that much of what the Günther School has created as regards the newly-stated connection between sound and gesture, music and dance, has been anticipated by others. Nevertheless I venture to assert: never before has music been presented in this organically formed unity, in the service of the rhythmical/dance elements.

This novel creative situation has been reached by means of two factors, which are both central to the rhythmical events at the Günther School. These are: gestural/musical improvisation with a percussion orchestra, and a sound orchestra. This is indebted to the sound orchestra of Wigman, and also, in its inner structure, fed by Asiatic sources. For anyone who – like the writer of these lines – has had the opportunity to see these two elements of Günther theory in practice, for him the times of unrestrained, interpretive psychology in the art of dance of the post-war years (i.e. 1919 onwards) are finally past. Then, one happily thought of being able to express in dance side by side Bach fugues, Schubert *Lieder*, the Theory of Relativity, and a Radetzky March. Instead he will gain an entirely new relationship to music which is organic for dance, similar in concept to that cultivated by the great masters of the Middle Ages up to the French ballet and its decadent successors in the nineteenth century. Indeed he will be able to examine this music much more thoroughly in terms of its specifically dance content. A teaching method which is as simple as it is ingenious will put him in a position for this: it is the *a priori* established unity of movement education and music education, as advocated in words, in writings, and through their actions by Dorothée Günther and by Carl Orff, the director of the music department of her school. In this plan of education, music and rhythm, instrument and melody, gesture and dance, all grow from *one* common root. In place of 'choreography', or dance arrangements, or the mechanical subdivision of the musical material into rhythmical 'membra disiecta' (sections), in which the 'spiritual connection between the parts' is absent, and instead of the domination of abstract ballet steps over the curve of the melody, over the harmonic base, and the instrumental colouring, there is homogeneous growth of the melodic body and of the spatial contour of dance. This growth is primarily promoted by nurturing improvisation, which extends to the sound-maker just as much as to the dancer. From the practical demands of the sound/dance improvisation there results, as if spontaneously, the construction of the orchestra for dance, which reaches from the most primitive stages of the creation of rhythmical accent (stamping, beating, rattling) up to the most sophisticated melodic synthesis (recorder, celesta, glockenspiel).

The orchestra for dance at the Günther School is in fact the first European orchestra that has creatively assimilated the ideas of the East. The vast multiplicity of the Burmese percussion orchestra (the so-called gamelan orchestra), whose beautiful recordings on disc, together with the theoretical interpretation given them by Curt Sachs, have been publicised far too little. The variety of the Asiatic styles of playing within the families of drum, gong, and bell, together with the primitive sharpness and clarity of diatonic flute melodies – these can all be found in the functioning of this astonishing Günther School orchestra, whose players are young girls, who alternately play, dance, and conduct. Even conduct! It is amazing what this School can achieve through educational improvisation, especially in the case of musical sign language. To budding conductors no better training can be recommended for overcoming the inhibitions caused by civilisation and a lack of gestural expression than the method of conductor's improvisation at this School.[1] From the astonishing results of this method it really becomes clear how vital is the connection between music and movement for the creative musician. His intellectual isolation would be easier to cure by means of this practice than with the aid of the obscure ideology of 'utility music', the contents of which are mostly not strong enough to be used for other purposes than as say that of a 'musical sharing' in which the participants respond in a very intellectual way. Of course, that music at the

---

1 This educational significance of conducting was recognised much earlier by Jaques-Dalcroze and also assumes an important place in the curriculum of Hellerau School at Laxenburg.

Günther School belongs conceptually to another planet than say the music of German polyphony. But it is indigenous music for dance, as say 'stantipes' and 'ductia' were in the dances of the Middle Ages, and it is suitable as material for 'utility music' – not in the political sense – but in the sense, say, of being of use as was the lute music of the Renaissance. As such it would have a claim to be thoroughly considered, even by creative musicians whose work is more rooted in the metaphysical.

VOL. IV, NO. 1, JUNE 1931

On Dance Criticism

Alfred Brasch

Last year's appeal for the foundation of a dance critics' association has brought to the fore yet another question which is really a current issue for dancers. In particular, since the existence of concert-dance and the so-called New Dance, there have been no end of complaints about the critics' lack of judgement. The lack of discrimination of critics who have been appointed, rather than having a 'calling', has given rise to protests against many a dance review and also the thought of forming an association of critics which should certainly be something like an exclusive club for those who have a vocation.

But first just one question: is this trouble concerning criticism just something peculiar to today's dance or does it not exist in all fields of artistic work? You only need to look at the papers once to see what nonsense is being served up almost daily on the critical page of local and even nationally-read papers. In most cases this will never be able to be changed since the decision about the occupant of the responsible post lies, in the end, with the publishers of the newspaper. They rarely appoint their critics according to exclusively artistic considerations and their own objectively proven judgement; in most cases they have to depend on someone else's opinion or on the title and beautiful turn of phrase of the applicant.

When a critic is taken on in this way and is set to work without understanding his field to any desirable degree, then subjective impressions which he is not able to control will probably characterise his criticism; this will thereby become useless, though not absolutely in every case. We shall take this point up again later. But then he is in a fix: if he writes 'bad' this starts up the complaints and with good reason since the poor thing cannot give objective grounds for his disapproval; but if he writes 'good' – then the dancers do indeed rejoice over the prophet and cut out the beautiful and the most poetically gushing sentences for their publicity. So long as dancers themselves do not consider it beneath their dignity to hawk such rubbish about (for time and again one finds dance evenings of prominent or less than prominent groups and soloists announced in such tasteless, conceited and, as already said, seemingly worthless clippings) then, the longer the absolutely hateful slating review will also quite definitely exist as just another side of that flattery over which so many people rejoice.

The crucial question concerning who has a calling to be a critic is difficult to determine by means of minimum requirements, but above all it should not be external things which are the decisive factor. Recently, it has slipped my mind where and by whom, it was even demanded that the dance critic should at least have contact with the dancers, should be generally familiar with their work and with the personality of a dancer. A pure critic who would come to this from the outside quite without any contact with artists or with dance, except for the performance in hand – therefore with the judgement of the 'perfect spectator' – is declared to be almost an impossibility. There is some truth in this. Every artistic expression presupposes an ability to abstract, without which it can neither happen nor be understood. Every artistic field creates its own language, which is determined by the logic of its material and spiritual form. Now, the artist is one who can speak or under-stand this language, who can grasp its form and, of course, understand its logic as the organising principle of this world. This person can be both the creator as well as the judge who is looking on. And whether this person is artistic or not is what forms the parting of the ways. Just as there are dancers who are only 'dancers', meaning those who have learnt something and use it, so there are also journalists who work out phrases about dance or any other art form and are the offenders with euphoric or satanic 'reviews'.

But those others who once, some time, experienced the unique nature of art and ever since then belonged in its world, they – dancing or writing – will serve the art. Just those 'non-dancing' but artistic people whom we may say really ought to be rejected as critics could be allotted an important task because their judgement is not yet corrupted by close familiarity. A long time ago we agreed on, and tailored, a host of verbal formulae and forms, including those from the New Dance, which are now available for use by all critics when looking at a work. But these are considered to be beyond discussion. This new critical language of dance, like that of musical expressionism, because of the isolation of its development is not compelling enough for the general public. It is perhaps this language which still in great part has to be opened up to the new dance movement? But which of us, who counts himself part of that 'establishment', has dared risk an answer to that? For this last type of criticism we need an artistic person who does not know anything about the conventions of our art and is completely impartial.

Moreover we should think whether the aptitude of the dance critic should be discussed. But firstly something else is more important, and this reminder is meant for the dancers, those who are being criticised: think on the fact that in the sight of fair art critics it is only art that matters; good craftsmanship and personal charm are all very well but leave the good critics simply indifferent; what the female dancer needs instead of sex appeal is art. If you listen calmly to the sincere critic, you do not have to capitulate to what is simply the vanity of shop-talk from one who does not know what he ought about positions and movements, since that serves no purpose. But think above all about this, that every phrase about 'the bewitching music of charming limbs' and 'talented 20-year-olds' (who is in doubt that they were also once 20 years old?) undermines the appreciation of dance – educate your critics! – such a phrase not only insults you by its lack of judgement, but also harms you by that lack, more perhaps than a scathing review which is well-written – and which you may have deserved.

VOL. II, NO. 2, JULY 1929

Dance Photography

Charlotte Rudolph

Only a short time ago the dancer had to be satisfied with the posed picture. The dancer was forced to take up a position and to hold it. The photographic shot required the position to be maintained longer than the dancer was used to. Thus expression and movement were influenced. In addition it was only possible to photograph a 'principal moment' (see below), and this was torn out of the dance as a whole as an isolated movement. Photography of actual dance is only possible when it takes place during the motion.

Dance photography is therefore the representation of the motion of the dancer in picture form, that means that the dancer dances during the shooting. The dancer dances his dance, improvises, jumps, turns etc. Every moment can be photographed! Even if every moment does not make a good picture it is still interesting in the study of the way the movement happens. But it should not be implied here that senseless snapping will bring about results. In order to realise the right moment one must be able to totally empathise with each different rhythm of the dancer and have above all things an understanding of dance.

I break the dance down into *principal moments* and *transitional moments*. Under principal moments I understand, for example, the moment of greatest tension, the moment of greatest relaxation, the moment of suspension. By transitional moments I mean the moment of changing from one movement into another, a moment which has come out of a leading moment, a moment taken from a short rhythm. The principal moments are relatively easier to photograph, with the exception of a leap, turn and similar things. The transitional moments demand an even more concentrated synchrony. The photographer has not only got to feel himself in the role of the dancer, but he must sense *in anticipation,* since due to the mediation of the brain the eye sees the moment later than the camera. This fraction of a second can be all it takes to catch the wrong moment.

The dancer's movement is subject to spatial laws. As a result the dance picture should represent the spatial effects of the movement. In the photographic reproduction the 'perspective effect' and 'distortion' are nearly the same. As long as the dancer dances in the sideways dimension it is easy to get a good picture, and the same applies when the dancer moves his body on the diagonals. However, with widely sweeping movement in the diagonal direction foreshortenings can occur. If the dancer moves forward, head back, arms stretched out in front, the hands become too big, the arms shortened, the head too small in proportion. This is the controversial point. Some reject the shot because of its 'distortion', others are pleased with the 'perspective reproduction'. Probably in the course of time views will alter again in this field.

The dance picture should reproduce the characteristic movement of the dancer. I have known the dancer to be characterised more strongly by the transitional moments than by the principal moments. The principal moment gives a firm, definite movement, which depending on the disposition of the dancer turns out more imaginatively, simply or gymnastically. The transitional moment is the carrier of personal nuance. By way of an example I would like to mention that in the case of dancers whose talents lie in their statuesque qualities the principal moments contribute more strongly to the characterisation than do the transitional ones; in the case of lyrically talented dancers the transitional moments tend to be stronger. Of course principal and transitional moments can be equally characteristic. Grasping the essential thing at the right time and ignoring the minor thing is the precondition for capturing the characteristic essence of a dance in a picture.

The dance picture should reproduce the material of the dancer's costume correctly, because even these materials have expressive value. One must be able to distinguish flowing silk from heavy satin or thick brocade in the picture. I had to completely dismantle my entire photographic technique in order to fulfil all the requirements which dance photography asks for.

As I have already mentioned, it is also possible to produce shots for the study of the way the movement happens. These pictures can be of educational value for the young and youngest dancers. From these they can be shown where their instability and mistakes lie. For me personally it is extraordinarily interesting to gain an insight into the development of dance, not only of individual dancers but also of whole schools, by comparing my materials collected over the years. An overview on this scale could hardly have been possible with posed shots.

VOL. III, NO. 3, NOVEMBER 1930

Concerning Dance Costume

Georg Kirsta

As nothing remained even before the war of those Bakstian dance costume designs except as a few fragments of beautiful nudes, the creation of new dance costumes was a burning topical question. These new costumes, which had taken the place of the faded ones of Bakst, were created using ideas from the cubist style in painting of that time. Cardboard, wire, tin and canvas were in favour. To confess to using more noble fabric like satin and silk was, at that time, in extremely bad form. That was an age which thrived on combat.

A few years later the human body broke out unchanged and as before, in spite of our endeavours with tubes of thin metal sheeting and scant linen. (Karneval[1] gladly took on the cardboard and tin supply.) The period when brassières and bloomers were the dance costume had arrived. These emancipated underclothes were quite touching as the clothing of female dancers – touching, because the next logical step had undeniably to be naked people in the dance, thus a wild and at the same time uninhibited man, a kind of choreographic *Wandervogel*.[2] We will intentionally overlook this period – out of love for the true dance theatre. Sometimes it seemed as if the dance costume was growing into something monstrous for the sake of 'total spatial arrangement', as it was called in specialist circles. Many metres of material accompanied *one* dancer onto the stage, and, although the title of the dance was very sophisticated, the performer made the comic impression of a textile tamer. But now this bad dream has come to an end.

These days a bathing suit often happens to be the single uncompromising basis of a dance costume (just like the basic design of the hooped skirt was in the eighteenth century). But yet again only for that type of solo dance which takes place in a realistic setting – house, yard, garden. This factor becomes of secondary importance as soon as we step onto the stage,

1 Probably the name of a firm dealing with outrageous clothing for carnival time.
2 See Chapter One, Editorial I, for an explanation of the term *Wandervogel*.

because the dancer is performing here in a separate unreal world: music, stage set, coloured light. The dancer, therefore, has now to be dressed taking these three phenomena into consideration.

Now that we have overcome the slimming diet in the field of dance costume caused by abstraction, let us return to the sweetly scented treasure chest of 1870. Glorious things are in there: tightly fitting bodices, frills, sequins and lace (the latter must first be thoroughly bleached and enlarged so that *our* eyes can see it). And instead of the heroic medals of the past – many spangles. In a word: borrowings. And because there are other arts – the higher ones – which do it, we do not need to be ashamed of our loan.

The greatest achievement of our work: the rediscovery of the tailored cut without which a good dance costume is unthinkable (please do not think this only means a 'perfect fit'!). The cut reproduces the basic choreographic line of the prevailing type of dance; the colour of the fabric determines the degree of warmth in the dance, and the modest ornament (yes indeed) shapes or rather underlines the cadences of the movements. These are incredibly important, they must 'sit' there precisely and above all tally with the music. (Consider for a start the fine, old military uniforms: the distinction of their pot-pourri of trimmings and braid and their relationship to musical rhythm even if in a completely alien field.)

It is hopeless to lay down any directions for the development of the dance costume today – for they would all come to nothing. What I said before about the cut, colour and the musically-derived ornament for the body has quite proved its worth in all the times when the dance costume flourished. And in spite of this, temporary exaggerations in one of these aspects of a costume can recur at any time. These excesses are justifiable because they have arisen from what has been deeply felt, as well as from the artistic tendencies which are heightened at that moment.

CHAPTER FIVE

Personalities – Reviews – Events

Editorial V

The Munich Dancers' Congress was the third gathering of the German dance community. The first congress, dominated by Laban, was held at Magdeburg after the Theatre Exhibition in summer 1927. Although there was controversy over Wigman's absence and no contribution from the classical school, nevertheless a number of well-known personalities took part both in the discussions and the performances. Amongst these were Hans Brandenburg, the writer; Egon Wellesz, the composer; Dr Niedecken-Gebhard, the theatre director; and Max Terpis, the dancer and choreographer. Solo performers included Magito, Skoronel and Kreutzberg, while Feist and Bodenwieser presented group works. The congress was also notable for the performances of three contrasting and original works choreographed by Laban. The first, *Ritterballett,* was a narrative set in medieval Germany to a Beethoven score. The second presentation, *Nacht,* was probably one of the most *avant-garde* choreographies of its time. It was a satirical comment on urban society using mundane movement and an innovative score of jazz and *musique concrète.* The third piece, *Titan,* was a visionary work for a large cast, later produced as a movement choir.

The Magdeburg Congress was followed a year later by the Second Congress, held in Essen. Organised primarily by Kurt Jooss, this event attracted an even larger number of participants. It was here that Laban presented his notation publicly for the first time. The education of the dancer and the provision of a state college of higher education for dance were also major topics of discussion. Of the performances, Wigman's was commented on as outstanding.

The Third Congress, in Munich in 1930, started in a different economic climate, 1929 being the year of the worldwide financial collapse. Unemployment, already a problem for dancers, became a desperate reality for many more. However, as Schlee points out in his article, far too little time was spent on finding solutions to this rapidly escalating crisis.

One topic of interest which surfaced at this congress was the connection between amateur dance and socialism. Martin Gleisner spoke of his work with young manual and office workers in Gera, Thüringen and in Berlin where he had produced large movement and speech choirs.

As at previous congresses, performances played a major part in Munich. Audiences had anticipated Talhoff's *Totenmal (Memorial)* would be a highlight. However, it proved to be a complete failure.

Mary Wigman found it hard to adapt her work to Talhoff's constantly changing guidelines and her choreography had progressed very slowly. She did not have much experience in directing large groups of people (there were 50 dancers); furthermore the dance content seemed to be completely overpowered by the spoken word. Schlee was not alone in his condemnation of the production and its wastage of much needed funds. Most critics agreed that *Totenmal* was far too simplistic. It seemed an anachronism from the early Expressionist days when emotional intensity completely ruled over precision and form. *Totenmal* was Mary Wigman's greatest failure since the beginning of her independent career in 1919.

The Third Congress ended in acrimony. One contributory factor was the uneasy relationship between the disciples of Wigman and Laban. Mary Wigman throughout her career emphasised her indebtedness to her teacher, Laban, but it was more difficult for her pupils to take the same view. She was surrounded by a group of successful young artists, such as Harald Kreutzberg, Gret Palucca and Yvonne Georgi. Her school was internationally famous, her career as a dancer and choreographer was unequalled in Germany and it was beginning to expand to America. Mary Wigman in 1930 was the high priestess of the New Dance.

Laban's role in the dance world was of a very different nature. His performing career ended in 1926 and his choreographic efforts since 1927 had mostly been directed towards large works for amateurs. Therefore, on a theatrical level, he was no rival to Mary Wigman. And yet he was appointed to Max Terpis's post at the State Theatres in Berlin in 1930.

In 1929, in a tribute to Laban on his fiftieth birthday, Mary Wigman recognised him as her mentor and, however uneasy their relationship was in respect of positions and jobs and leadership of the New German Dance, she never withdrew her gratitude.

A number of articles in *Schrifttanz* focus on some of the outstanding individuals of the period. They show the range of styles, ideals and backgrounds which made early twentieth century European theatre dance such a diverse phenomenon.

Anita Berber could not be any further removed from the wholesome image of the 'Dalcrozienne' performing harmonious rhythmical exercises in beautiful surroundings which, after all, was still a persisting image of the German dance. Her short career was riddled with scandal and ended tragically, when she was only 29 years old, with her death in a tuberculosis hospital in Berlin in 1928. Anita Berber was a 'Nackttänzerin', a nude dancer; her world of cabaret, seedy nightlife, drugs and homosexuality was one treated with a mixture of fascination and great suspicion by the bourgeoisie of the Weimar Republic. She achieved fame, especially after her appearance in Fritz Lang's film *Dr Mabuse,* but few people were willing to take her seriously as an artist.

The review in *Schrifttanz,* published posthumously, tries to look behind the image. Anita Berber's actual dance is described and analysed in terms of movement and expression. What emerges is the portrait of an artist with great concern for the form and content of her art.

This chapter closes with appreciations of three outstanding personalities of the theatre. Josef Lewitan, a dance critic and editor of *Der Tanz,* opened his article on the Diaghilev Ballet as follows:

> Whilst this issue was being printed, we received the news that Diaghilev had died from a stroke. Diaghilev's unique personality had shaped the style of the modern Russian Ballet. Diaghilev was a Maecenas, equally forceful as artistic initiator and organiser. With unerring certainty he discovered new talents. He succeeded in secur- ing the co-operation of the most gifted Russian and French artists. The outcome of his life's work is the international recognition of Russian art, and of the ballet in particular. With his death we have lost one of the strongest and most interesting personalities of modern art.

The news of Anna Pavlova's death two years later prompted Laban to write an appreciation of her life and artistry. This underlines Laban's relationship with ballet. Far from being antagonistic, an attitude often attributed to him, he saw himself as a part of the ongoing tradition of dance.

Armin Knab's review of Wigman's *Visionen* is an example of the new, more analytical style of writing which began to appear in the mid-1920s, most dance criticism in the early twentieth century having been highly subjective and purely impressionistic. He not only described Wigman's style, but also looked at her work in a historical context. Mary Wigman does not represent the typical woman of her time, she is not the 'anonymous modern girl' of the 1920s and early 1930s. What her dance is representative of, however, is the German concern with intellectual content in art. Knab values Wigman's serious approach, but he feels it has removed itself too far from 'the essential movement quality of dance, which is needed to educate the audiences to honour what is natural and beautiful'.

VOL. III, NO. 3, NOVEMBER 1930

The Munich Dancers' Congress

Alfred Schlee

After a space of four months we can try to look at the results of the dance congress more objectively. The distance of time corrects first impressions. Annoyance, applause, saturation and boredom no longer touch us directly and have half disappeared from our memory. We do not want to bring back what has been forgotten nor, on this occasion, do we want to deal with individual performances, good or bad, but only to try to record the key experiences of this past summer's events.

Initially, the disappointing outcome of the congress causes us to ask ourselves again what we had expected from the congress and similar events. In the first issue of this year's *Schrifttanz* I tried to give a general view of the situation of dance in our time. My statement outlined the task which ought to be given to the review of a significant gathering of specialists which this year's congress offered. This task consisted of no more and no less than the formation of a union of dancers. From the point of view of organisation, this is necessary in order to fight the constantly deteriorating economic difficulties and, from an artistic point of view, in order to give unity to the many individual efforts of new and older forms of dance. Out of this senseless coexisting medley, we could create a universally recognised foundation. However, the congress did not even succeed in setting itself this objective. The essential aim was missed. Indeed, there were some interesting speeches and a number of speakers who made strong personal impressions. But most of it consisted of statements of well-known facts. There were no debatable issues and no inspiration for further development. Possibly the only exception was presented by the depressing statistics concerning social conditions and the resulting positive involvement of the Catholic Church which was represented in such a masterly and perfect way that the astonishment only ceased when the congress was already over and therefore the questions arising in this area were not dealt with either.[1]

In Essen,[2] work had been made difficult by the stark contrast of opposing views. Ill-feeling had been created by some inconsiderate speakers and their demagogic manners. This time, however, the leadership of the congress with its exaggerated tendency towards bureaucracy stifled all attempts which could have led to further development. What was missing was an

---

1 The meaning of this sentence is not completely clear: 'Einzige Ausnahmen waren vielleicht die bedrückende Statistik über die soziale Lage und das positive Eingreifen der katholischen Kirche, *die so meisterhaft und formvollendet vertreten war...*'
2 The Second Dancers' Congress in 1928.

inspiring personality who could have united the people. Everybody was too careful and held back instead of pushing ahead. And especially this time, preliminary conditions had been ideal. Dancers had never been so willing to work for a common cause as they had been this time. The wish to do so had been present everywhere, everybody had been waiting for the first step: all had been inspired, all but the leadership of the congress.[3] They did not manage to transform this latent feeling into fruitful motivation. A missed opportunity which will never return!

Only one word about the performances. They proved that the system by which they were organised does not work. Performances cannot be arranged on the basis of proportional representation.[4] By using mere administrators instead of an artistically responsible leadership, all considerations of quality which would have been crucial for the composition of the festival's programme had been brushed aside. It was an irony that after such a confusing mixture of performances there were still some unsatisfied people who complained about discrimination against some group or another. They have as little understanding of the purpose of dance festivals as the organisers had.

If we single out *Totenmal* as the only work we are looking at, the reason for this is that it should have presented the central focus of the congress and of the festival. However, another reason is that on the advice of the brilliant specialists and because of our trust in Mary Wigman's co-operation, we had greatly supported the choric work of art. Therefore, we are obliged to acknowledge that, not only were we deeply disappointed, but we regard *Totenmal* as having brought disrepute upon the idea of the ritual theatre. We deeply regret that Mary Wigman, especially after the masterpiece *Schwingende Landschaft*, wasted her talents on this amateurish creation. However, we are not merely dealing with an ordinary artistic failure. At a time when a number of theatres are fighting for their survival, one single work consumed the amount of money which would have secured a theatre's budget for an entire year. Our time, more than ever before, demands a strong sense of responsibility. Even the private Maecenas has no right to undermine our cultural standing by presenting such works as *Totenmal*.

Is it coincidence that we can conclude this report without actually having discussed artistic questions? The dance congress has done nothing to change the artistic situation. In spite of a number of good performances (even though most of these pieces were familiar), our pessimism was reinforced. Even such a striking artistic appearance as Dorothée Günther

---

3 Laban and Jooss, organisers of the 1927 and 1928 Congresses, were at Bayreuth choreographing the Tannhäuser *Bacchanale*. Their input was minimal.

4 In German: 'Festspiele lassen sich nicht paritätisch erzwingen'. Possibly the author means that each region or company was entitled to a certain amount of performance time.

with Maja Lex, whose discovery we have to credit the congress with, and about whom we hope to report on a different occasion, has not helped to correct our impressions.

During the congress, Kurt Jooss made a suggestion which went largely unnoticed. Instead of a fourth congress he would like to see workshops lasting several weeks, which rather than being festive occasions with large audiences, concentrate on the essential issues related to dance, which then would be dealt with in a co-operative, practical manner by committed specialists. We regard this proposition as the only way to make up for what the last congress failed to do or even destroyed.

VOL. III, NO. 1, APRIL 1930

.*Totenmal* and Dance

Hans Brandenburg

This year, the Third Dancers' Congress will take place in June in Munich and will be organised by the dance world in collaboration with the Chorische Bühne[1] as German Dance Week. As part of its programme there will also be a gala performance by the Chorische Bühne of Albert Talhoff's *Totenmal* (*Memorial*). This 'dramatic-choric vision for speech, dance and light' not only presents a great challenge to the choreographer – even this by itself is quite unique – but it also introduces a form in which the choric theatre and the dance theatre are one. This form might rescue the theatre as well as the dance out of their crises, by leading to a closer fusion of the two than has been achieved through opera. Certainly it is significant that Mary Wigman has dealt with the dance side, Adolf Linnebach with the lighting and technical arrangements, Bruno Goldschmitt with the masks and the scenery, and Karl Vogt with the rehearsal of the spoken parts. In this respect, all the individual tasks have been entrusted to specialists. But what is even more significant, indeed decisive, is that in the mind of the creator of this work, and within the work itself, all the individual parts already form a whole even before its first performance. It is also noteworthy that here a new type of professional artist is continuing what has been started by amateur groups. Further reasons are that the special choir has been transformed into a 'speech orchestra', the movement choir into a dramatic voice, modern lighting has become an instrument and a factor for creating space, and what

---

1 Chorische Bühne: here it is the name of a theatrical association. It is also a form of stage art which aims to give independent, yet equal, status to dramatic acting, movement and vocal choirs. The article will explain this in detail.

is most important, the unifying force of these means finds its origin in dance and dancers, in space in relation to time.

The *chorische Bühne* of the future can only come alive from a variety of old and new forms. For the first time, Talhoff creates a clear and definite realisation of one of these forms. In it, it is space itself which moves, which has sound and light, and thus becomes active. This, however, means danced theatre, not in the specialised theatre of dance, but in its most comprehensive meaning.[2] And it is this meaning which Talhoff confirms with his idea, with the universal spirit of *Totenmal*. He has realised that spiritual unity can only arise from dancing together, even though it is led by words. Unaffected by others, he keeps the different fields of expression apart: he does not want the dancer to speak nor does he want the actor to dance.

It is true that he wants to replace the usual actor with an actor who can dance, but because of the limitations of contemporary training, he still wants professional artists to remain within their specialist functions, and only come together in the overall structure of the whole work.

Talhoff himself has written the notation of the 'speech orchestra', as well as the supporting orchestra and the lighting. For the choreography he relies on Laban's dance notation and points out that he wants to show his commitment to this form of notation for the score.[3] Indeed, right from the beginning Laban's notation was envisaged as having the important potential for also recording the dramatic events. But where in Germany can we find a way of directing theatre which requires such notation, or rather, which would be worthy of it? *Totenmal,* however, is the first piece of drama, other than a pure dance work, which cannot be interpreted arbitrarily, for it does not become clear from the textbook alone, but requires a pre-written dance score to the same extent as it requires words and a musical score.

Talhoff's concept of it as dance is as an independent art with its own notation, but in his own script he can only use words as provisional means. He needs choreographers[4] to assist him, and they need the task set by him, so that for the first time a combined speech, light and dance score could come into being.

---

2 Brandenburg contrasts *Tänzerisches Theater* (which is the comprehensive form) with *Tanzbühne* (which is the specialised form). To some extent *Tänzerisches Theater* can be equated with *chorische Bühne*.

3 Not completely clear: '. . . und möchte sich ihr partiturisch verpflichtet fühlen.'

4 Here 'choreographer' means dance composer who is also a dance notator.

<u>VOL. II, NO. 4, DECEMBER 1929</u>

Rudolf von Laban on his Birthday

Mary Wigman

Rudolf von Laban's 50th birthday will be an occasion for many people to have a good look at this man's work, concentrating on the significance of his active output from a broader viewpoint than may generally be usual in relation to a person working in the fine arts.

Even though Laban's work cannot in any way be said to be complete at this time, after 30 years of work his essential characteristics and influence can be clearly recognised. His achievements, difficult to define in detail, nevertheless can be looked at on their own merit, no longer inextricably tied to his personality. Developed by himself, as well as by his pupils and followers, his work has today become the common property of the dance.

Present-day dancers, regardless of whether they have personally passed through Laban's school or not, respect and recognise in the name 'Laban' the start of a new era in the history of European dance. Although it may be proved historically that everything new was already there, the idea of dance with which we are concerned today first attained complete expression and form through the personality of Rudolf von Laban. He was the great discoverer and catalyst. He provided the foundation on which we, as dancers, whether knowingly or not, now base ourselves. He opened the gates to the world of dance which had been locked for us for so long. He taught us to recognise the nature of tension, the harmony and flow of movement sequences, the unity of body and rhythmic space. His principles, constructed meaningfully and organically, now form the basis of every physically oriented activity, from sport, through gymnastic exercise, to dance as an art form. Laban provided the experience of free improvisation, releasing for his pupils their creative forces. He freed the dance from enslavement to music and thus returned it to the independence of a true language of art. He investigated movement right down to its core and proved that the freed and released material could be given organic form in the composition of dance works.

If Laban was on the one hand a genius at improvisation, inexhaustible ideas, invention, stimulus and experiment, he often, while apparently playing, slid across from one level of dance discovery to another, for he was at the same time the rigorous researcher and theoretician who frantically and thoroughly tracked down the innate rules of dance movement. He never tired of starting, yet again, from another viewpoint, clarifying, arranging, constructing, until he penetrated the material whose vastness is scarcely comprehensible. Thirty years of untiring struggle to build a notation for dance, a visible and practical symbol of the organic and harmonic structure of movement.

This work stands, unimpeachable and visible for all time, as a record of total and selfless devotion to dance, and compels the comprehending and equally the uncomprehending among us to absolute respect and gratitude.

Laban's work, so far as it can be looked at objectively, detached from him personally, culminates in the two great emanations of his nature: in the form of the gifted discoverer and catalyst and also as the brilliant theoretician. The aspects of his works which are inseparable from his personality will eventually share the fate of all the performing arts: to sink and to be forgotten. Every dancer is aware of this fate and accepts it for the sake of those precious creative moments which connect him to life more deeply than words could ever express.

All of us who dance are more indebted to Laban's work than we realise while we are immersed in our own creative efforts.

As Rudolf von Laban's pupil and collaborator, I was able to travel a part of his creative way with him. I feel the need to thank him for what he has already achieved for dance and dancers. And if I may express a birthday wish for his future work: I hope that the ideas lying behind all his creations can be realised; great celebratory works which unite participants and spectators in a powerful shared experience.

VOL. IV, NO. 1, JUNE 1931

Kokain – An Attempt at an Analysis of Anita Berber's Dance

Joe Jencik

Curtain. On the floor, a nude body, an empty room filled with grey-blue dawn. Everywhere, the grandeur of death. Above, below, in front, behind, maybe in the motionless figure, too. Every detail as it was then, when she, hand in hand with an old friend, had entered the same room. A room in which, in great agony, she had to step over a man's body, who was lying there in a cocaine delirium.

This reminiscence of an episode of which her second husband had been the sad hero, is the beginning of one of her first creations, *Kokain*.

Deathly silence, no sign of consciousness. Obviously the first impact of this horrendous poison which paralyses everything. The soul fights hard to regain its former dominance over the body. Spasms, hardly visible, seize hold of the pale limbs, and the poor delirious creature unconsciously regains consciousness, for the love of life is indestructible. When the body sits up, the muscles resemble the swings of an elongated pendulum. The figure forms a bizarre tangle of flesh and two indescribable gaps as eyes, and a blood red opening as the mouth. The tangle unravels itself as if an order had been given by something in between reason and delirium. The dancer stands up, she is completely distant. She is a puppet caught in the no man's land between poison and lifeforce. Her blood chased by the will of nature aimlessly rushes through her veins. The poison, injected by the will of man, is merciless in its interference; it intrudes with a raw power into something which belongs to the great mystery of life. The body appears ridiculous and embarrassingly bloated. Its insides boiling, its outside icy. Imaginary screams, in surprise over sudden, uncertain visions, dissolve almost immediately. The dancer persecutes herself with the creations of her bizarre imagination. Life and poison in fierce battle, the heart finally grows weary, and the wild beast of cocaine addiction strangles its willing victim. The dancer throws herself to the floor. More agony – this time it is reminiscent of the tender sleep someone falls into having been freed from the depths of hell.

All this is performed with simple steps and natural, unstylised poses. Attitudes in this dance appear tragically broken, and arabesques are elongated so that they almost seem supernatural. The body rotating around its axis, languid, as if filmed in slow motion, then – suddenly like the crack of a whip – the almost sculptured *port-de-bras* comes to an abrupt end. Unexpected countermovements of the head, incompatible with the body's equilibrium. Positions of the feet: mostly in wide fourth, which accentuate the strange art of this unique dancer. Her entire technique follows the dynamics of her dream which, freed from gravity, dissolves the dancer's physicality into the finest shades of lightness. *Kokain* and *Morphium* are Anita Berber's most important and most personal creations, reminiscent of the great studies of a famous mime. She is a mime who knows the right moment to subordinate herself to the form of dance without surrendering to it completely.

VOL. II, NO. 3, AUGUST 1929

The Diaghilev Ballet

Joseph Lewitan

The performance of the Diaghilev Ballet during the Berlin Festival ought to be highly significant for the further development of German dance. The completeness of the programmes and the vitality of the dancers give such an

immense moral and aesthetic force to this company. It is virtually impossible for our rather self-satisfied and stagnant ideas of dance to compete
with the Russians'. Although these ideas are still represented, they no longer
represent the prevailing attitude. We have wasted years discussing what the
dance should be and thus manoeuvered ourselves into a cul-de-sac of over-
intellectualised theories of dance. In this climate any honest efforts nurtured
by years of pure enthusiasm are bound to be suffocated eventually. On the
other hand, Diaghilev's company is not burdened by theory. On the contrary,
it is abundant with talent and creativity. One senses immediately that this
path is rooted in old tradition, yet it has many possibilities, its horizon is
unlimited.

We can well predict, with a fair degree of accuracy, what the dancers of
Hellerau, Mary Wigman, Gret Palucca and others will show us in the near
future, without the risk of making a false prognosis. Diaghilev, on the other
hand, who does not seek the realisation of theories, but wants the dance
itself to be accomplished and who makes use of everything that is vibrant
and stimulating, always presents us with surprises. It is virtually impossible
to make any predictions. What he shows us today is completely different
from what the company performed only a few years ago. This season it is
neither *Tricorne* nor *Matelots* nor *Les Biches*. We must admit, however, that
what was shown seems less significant, less skilful, in comparison with the
previous creations.

Nevertheless we rejoice in this form of theatre, for its path is open and it
leads to the future – what matters is its spirit and its power, and eventually
these qualities always remain the driving force, even in the weaker performances.

This company, in which every day, without fail, each member practises
his *pliés, frappés, battements, ronds-de-jambe,* etc. at the barre and in the
centre, and which is so deeply rooted in the much despised ABC of the
classical dance; this company which is one hundred percent committed to
the 'rigid forms of a dead art', in reality is the most modern company in the
world. It is not the form of the movements which constitutes the difference
between old and modern, as imagined by so many confused dilettantes, but
what makes the theatre modern is its spirit. When forward looking directors,
painters, composers, conductors, ballet-masters and dancers work together,
and they all master their traditional skills, the result is bound to be modern.
And if necessary, movement sequences in the manner of Mary Wigman
(*Sacre du Printemps*) emerge easily without the need for specialised
training.

The ills of today's dance are not caused by a lack of new forms in the
movement. The problem is a question of attitude. In practice, the despised
old school provides the most fruitful technical basis for the creation of
dances. Because of its existence many valuable dance works have come to

life. And this is the most important lesson the performances of the Diaghilev Ballet can teach us.

As mentioned earlier the current programme is of a lower standard than previous ones created by Massine and Nijinska. Diaghilev almost exclusively presented the work of his latest ballet-master, Balanchine. Unfortunately, his imagination is not rich enough to create a full repertoire. It is only sufficient for limited tasks as it exhausts itself easily. His imagination did, however, reach a peak in the male ensemble work in *Chatte* and also in the duet for Lifar and Markova (or sometimes Nijinska) in *Prodigal Son*. Here Balanchine created moments of unprecedented beauty and expressiveness. I remember the *jeté* with which the son crosses the fence when he leaves his parent's house, and the deeply moving, unforgettable return of the repentant son. One sees the return of a morally defeated human being who rises from the ground to cling to the vertical figure of the father and to envelop himself in the open cloak of paternal love.

A few more beautiful moments from other dances choreographed by Balanchine remain in my memory – an adagio by Lifar and Nikitina from Stravinsky's *Apollo,* a tarantella from Rieti's *Bal* and various others. Nevertheless, far too often there is a sense of inadequate imagination, a certain misuse of acrobatic movements, uninspired sequences and stylistic mistakes. Still – and this has to be appreciated openly – there is a constant search, an urgent energy.

Bauhaus-like ideas in *Chatte,* Wigman-like ideas in *Sacre du Printemps,* an almost Fokine-like romanticism in *Bal,* successful drama in *Prodigal Son,* a modern yet pure interpretation of classicism in *Apollo* – how could we possibly give up faith and not believe in a great future simply because of a few minor shortcomings!

Everything that is valuable will remain in Balanchine's work, and everything else will disappear. For Diaghilev does not rest; already today he is encouraging his exceptional new talent, Serge Lifar, to be his ballet-master; maybe his tartar blood will impel him towards new revelations. Sooner or later the most modern of all Russian ballet-masters, the Muscovite Kassjan Golesowsky, will work for Diaghilev. This theatre will continue. The art it creates is alive, not dead.

Figure 13. Mary Wigman, 1930 (photo: Charlotte Rudolph, Dresden) in Aubel, Hermann & Marianne *Der künstlerische Tanz unserer Zeit*, Leipzig: Blaue Bücher, 1930

Figure 14. Essen Dancers' Congress, 1928. *Front row, l. to r.:* Olga Brandt-Knack, Heinrich Kröller, Max Terpis, Lizzie Maudrik, Gertrud Snell, Hans Brandenburg, Berthe Trümpy, Rudolf von Laban, Dussia Bereska, Alfred Schlee, Vera Skoronel,

Fritz Böhme, Manda von Kreibig. *Back row, l. to r.:* Harald Fürstenau, Aurel von Milloss, ?, Hertha Feist, Sigurd Leeder, Hanns Niedecken-Gebhardt, Kurt Jooss, ?, ?. (photo: Robertson, Berlin)

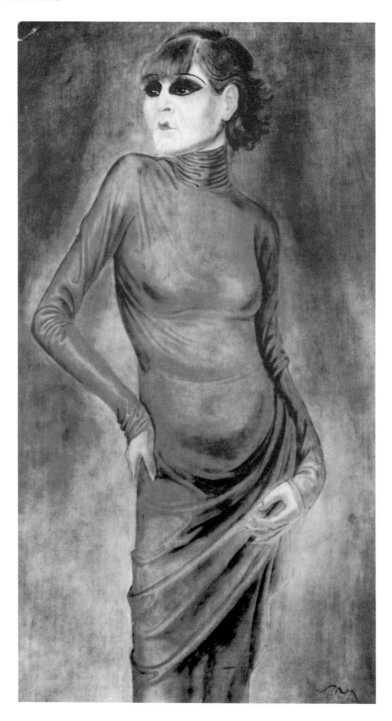

Figure 15. LEFT *Anita Berber* by Otto Dix, 1925 (photo: anon.) in Fischer, Lothar *Anita Berber/Tanz zwischen Rausch und Tod*, Berlin: Haude & Spenersche Verlagsbuchhandlung, 1984

Figure 16. ABOVE Vera Skoronel's Dance Group (photo: Suse Byk, Berlin)

Figure 17. TOP LEFT Tanzbühne Laban in his dance tragedy *Gaukelei*, 1923 (photo: K. Schellenberg) in *Die Schönheit*, 1926

Figure 18. ABOVE Rudolf von Laban and Gert Ruth Loeszer, 1925 (photo: anon., from F. Klingenbeck)

Figure 19. LEFT Rudolf von Laban and Berlin State Opera dancers, 1930 (photo: anon., from Martin Gleisner Collection)

Figure 20. Harald Kreutzberg and Yvonne Georgi in *Stravinsky Suite*, 1928 (photo: Robertson, Berlin), in Fischer, Hans W. *Körper, Schönheit und Körperkultur*, Berlin: Deutsche Buchgemeinschaft, 1928

Figure 21. Max Terpis *Der Letzte Pierrot* (*The Last Pierrot*), 1929 (photo: Robertson, Berlin), in Freund, Liesel (ed.) *Monographien der Ausbildungsschulen für Tanz und tänzerische Körperbildung*, Berlin: Alterthum Verlag, 1929

VOL. IV, NO. 1, JUNE 1931

Anna Pavlova

Rudolf von Laban

A dance that filled a whole life suddenly ended. The dance of a chosen one. In her appearance, in her life and in her art she seemed to be illuminated by a special glow. She seemed to have entered into a space that only exists in our dreams. Anna Pavlova made this space into a visible and tangible reality that gave so much joy and inspiration to a great many people. Not only in very special moments did she present us with her unique glow but she permeated space and time in every step, in every pose, even in the smallest and most insignificant of gestures. Her language was dance. Her art, like no other, demands the commitment of the whole person. It means that complete self-discipline and sacrifice are required if one chooses to practice this form of art.

Anna Pavlova tells us in her memoirs how, as a child, she was already totally fascinated by the dance. Her play was dance, her dreams were dance. She danced to compete with the blossoming of flowers and the rhythm of animals. She danced in her garden and she danced in the forest, she danced for the moon and she danced for the sun even long before she was accepted into ballet school. Those who knew her are aware that she did not make up a biographical fairy-tale for the enlightenment of future generations. She was born a dancer; it was not, as the saying goes, her second nature, but her first, her original nature. Already as a child it meant sacrifice and anxiety, for she was too small, too fragile and too young for the Imperial Ballet School. Finally she was accepted, then another sacrifice followed, one happily made with a desirable but long-term goal. This sacrifice was the hard discipline of the body and the monastic isolation of the ballet school. Her goal seemed to be too far away. It was a dream, a vague idea that only became crystallised at a much later stage. But the obvious, conscious and nearest goal was not just grace and suppleness, it was something else. Those waves, the waves of the body were an awakening, a baring of an inner core, not only of the person but of a strange, distant world. This world is inherent in all that is beautiful and inspiring and in all that gives happiness.

In no other art is the danger of not transcending the technical so pronounced as it is in dance. The concentration on function and physique can lead to a narcissistic identification with the body. The adoration of skill can have a paralysing effect. It is a very special gift not to succumb to this danger. Anna Pavlova was blessed with the gift to dissolve that rigidity, to transform it into something abundant with vitality and mystery. Therefore she was a perfect instrument ready for the revolutionary movement ideas proposed by the young Fokine. Fokine had been one of the first to fight against the rigidity of the classical ballet.

Anna Pavlova was already unequalled in her mastery of sylph-like lightness and grace when she explored the areas that characterised the new art of dance. She encountered new rhythms and the abundance of natural expressiveness. This newness met with the solid foundation of her tradition, the two merging in rich and magnificent synthesis.

During numerous journeys across the world Anna Pavlova gradually absorbed different dance material. But it was always harmonised with her own nature, her airiness that was so characteristic of the way she moved. The dances with which she awakened our enthusiasm were not all created by herself. As a real artist, she loved to pay tribute to the work itself, to show her empathy with the artist's creation. It would have never occurred to her, in her childlike modesty on the one hand and her subtle sophistication on the other, to confuse emotional outburst or acrobatic feats with the real art of dance. She was in awe of the laws of dance composition without ever becoming a slave to them. In dances that Fokine created for Pavlova, she demonstrated her superior artistry, her unique way of expression.

In relentless daily training, she not only maintained her skill at the highest level but continually improved it. The expression of her soul in harmony with the movements of her body were deeply touching. With her special sensitivity as a performing artist she joined ranks with the greatest singers and actors in the world. Thus she ennobled the dance and assured it a recognition which in our times is not so easily earned. Everything the most recent generation of dancers has striven for with great effort she already had perfected. She treated her achievements as a gift so natural that she did not seek to draw special attention to them. They were merely a means to an end – to dance – to express herself, to communicate the joy of an art for which she had become the high priestess. And this is where her greatness lies and why we will never forget her. She elevated the dance to a form of enlightenment even in a world which is covered by a veil of grief and torn apart by demons.

Today we think of her enchanting personality, the memory of her last performance remains with us. It is a memory of something that cannot be described with words but only through dance. Words can never be more than a pale representation of what she had to offer us. This dancer perfected the pure art of dance in such a way that no one ever thinks to ask about her methods or the titles and plots of her dances. This happened to many of us with the well known *Dying Swan*. The sinking and gliding, the rising and trembling were no expiration, no ending. The emotion stirred was not grief, not sadness. It was a fleeting symbol of the ephemeral, yet eternal, process of life.

Thus we are touched by her death beyond which her unforgettable life of a dancer shines on.

VOL. II, NO. 3, AUGUST 1929

Mary Wigman: *Visionen*

Armin Knab

The first dance is called *Ceremonial Figure.* An orange crinoline, a severe eastern mask. Conscious, capricious movements, minimal life, an awakening figure, the East is near. The sounds of the gong ring as if initiated by the movements of the hands, they are dance gestures that have become audible. In the second dance, *Dream Figure,* a climax has already been reached. The dancer appears like an exotic flower, grey on the outside, a deep red, the colour of pain, trying to burst from the inside, in between a body the colour of ivory. The face, distorted by pain, the eyes burning, is the embodiment of human suffering. Sometimes we are no longer reminded of the human form, grey leaves move like ghosts, the material of the costume seems to be driven by its own impulses. The monotonous sounds of a flute, a tuneless piano, together they banish the figure into a subhuman sphere from which she cannot escape.

The *Ceremonial Figure* of the third dance presents an unforeseen change; we see a green and golden cloak, trailing behind her, and beneath it we see a short, black tunic costume. In this dance, too, the body is an almost invisible force inside the voluminous garment reaching for infinity.

The *Witch Dance* presents another climax. Horror becomes rational form. A red and silver costume, a terrifying mask, reminiscent of Japanese ghosts, a curly, woollen wig. Strange hissing sounds are mirrored by convulsive movements, arms are transformed into snakes, a satanic, non-human instinct seems to inspire the gestures. The crouching figure triumphantly draws circles around herself, hands and feet following the same rhythms.

The purple ghost of the *Apparition* fills the space with long veils which magically arrange themselves into ceremonial shapes. The face becomes an empty surface from which the black hollows of the eyes cry out.

The *Space Figure* is not, as might have been expected, a clearly defined figure in a clearly defined space, but a bearer of a red flag, which sometimes wraps around the body, or again unfolds into infinity. Ecstacy persists and eventually leads to the figure's downfall.

Is the dance the most recent of the arts? Mary Wigman completes the period of Expressionism even though its peak had been reached around 1900. Her style cannot provide the basis for an ongoing school in the traditional sense; for communication in the new dance culture is free and direct. Mary Wigman refuses to stress her femininity, to adulterate her dance with naïve eroticism. This aspect she shares with Isadora Duncan, yet she does not merely use the body as a form of beauty in motion, she also exploits the expressive character of her costumes. In her world we do not find beauty for its own sake, nor Greek ideals, but the demonic, the dark side, the terrifying, springing mostly from oriental sources.

Her movement sequences, too, are oriental in character. On the one hand, they belong to a certain period in art which is inspired by ecstacy alone, on the other hand they resemble the ancient and timeless rhythms of Indian dance. Mary Wigman's art seems to fluctuate between these two poles. One can feel clearly that some of her movement sequences are directed by the intellect, yet others cannot be comprehended by logic alone.

It is strange that Mary Wigman's career should have blossomed in our time – the anonymous, modern girl always found in groups is her direct antithesis. If we dare use the term *Jugendstil,*[1] it is the spirit of this movement which is most akin to Mary Wigman's art. The essence of *Jugendstil* was not merely an expression of youth, but the emergence of an anti-bourgeois mood overladen with powerful emotions. Beardsley, Toorop, Munch, Poe, Maeterlinck, Meyerlink – all these great individuals managed to tame some sombre demons inside them and transform them into figures of brilliance and clarity.

This way of rationalising emotion is a truly German characteristic of art. In Romanic and Slavic cultures the strong influence of serious theoretical thought is far less prevalent. The German, on the other hand, who is not a dancer by nature, needs intellectual content in order to find meaning in dance.

In Mary Wigman's case, her personality fulfils this criterion. It is on her level, not the despised level of entertainment, that the German art of dance sought to build its foundations. This new art took the shape of serious dance recitals which strove for unusual materials, emotional depth and a theatrical content. What is needed, however, is a return to the essential movement quality of dance, to educate the audiences to honour what is natural and beautiful.

1 *Jugendstil* means literally style of youth.

APPENDIX I

List of Contents of Schrifttanz

VOL. I, NO. 1, JULY 1928

Schlee, Alfred, *Editorial*

Laban, Rudolf von, *Basic Principles of Movement Notation* (Grundprinzipien der Bewegungsschrift)

Böhme, Fritz, *A Chapter from the History of Written Dance* (Ein Kapitel aus der Geschichte der Choreographie)

Brandenburg, Hans, *Written Dance and the Theatre* (Schrifttanz und Bühne)

Maudrik, Lizzie, *Written Dance and Ballet* (Schrifttanz und Ballett)

Wagner-Régeny, Rudolf, *New Bases for Musical Theory as the Result of Research into Written Dance* (Neue Grundzüge der musikalischen Theorie als Ergebnis der Schrifttanzforschung)

Proceedings of The German Association for Written Dance (Mitteilungen der deutschen Gesellschaft für Schrifttanz)

Insert

Two notated exercises with music, excerpts from *Don Juan* (Laban)

VOL. I, NO. 2, OCTOBER 1928

Laban, Rudolf von, *Dance Composition and Written Dance* (Tanzkomposition und Schrifttanz)

Gleisner, Martin, *Written Dance and Amateur Dance* (Schrifttanz und Laientanz)

Sandt, Alfred, *Dance Notation and Written Dance of the 16th Century* (Die Tanzschrift und der Schrifttanz des 16. Jahrhunderts)

Galpern, Lasar, *Dance in its Time* (Die Zeit und der Tanz)

Paquet-Léon, C. von, *The Problem of Notation for Social Dance* (Das Problem der Tanzschrift für den Gesellschaftstanz)

Laban, Rudolf von, *The Development of Laban's Notation* (Die Entwicklung der Bewegungsschrift Laban)

News from Theatre Dance (vom Bühnentanz)
Proceedings of The German Association for Written Dance (Mitteilungen der
deutschen Gesellschaft für Schrifttanz)
Dancers' Congress in Essen – Report

Insert
Kinetogram of *Yale Blues*

VOL. II, NO. 1, JANUARY 1929

Kirsta, Georg, Costume sketch for *Pulcinella* on front cover
Kirsta, Georg, *Tomorrow's Ballet* (Ballett von Morgen)
Böhme, Fritz, *Margaret of Austria's Dance Book/On the History of Dance
Notation* (Das Tanzbuch der Margarethe von Österreich/Zur Geschichte
der Tanznotation)
Snell, Gertrud, *Foundations for a General Theory of Dance, Part I* (Grund-
lagen einer allgemeinen Tanzlehre)
Schlee, Alfred, *Problems in the Relationship between Music and Dance*
(Schwierigkeiten zwischen Musik und Tanz)

Discussion (Diskussion)
Algarotti, *About Ballets* (Von den Balletten)
Trümpy, Berthe, *Reply to Lasar Galpern's Article 'Dance in its Time'* (Zum
Aufsatz 'Der Tanz und die Zeit' von Lasar Galpern)

Music and Book Reviews (Noten und Bücher)
Musik für Tänzer (Music for Dancers), Universal Edition
Wiener-Doucet-Album, Universal Edition
Günther: *Rhythmische Grundübungen* (Rhythmical Exercises), Delphin
Verlag
Martin Gleisner: *Tanz für Alle* (Dance for All), Hesse und Becker

News Items (Notizen)
Proceedings of the German Association for Written Dance (Mitteilungen der
deutschen Gesellschaft für Schrifttanz)

Laban, Rudolf von, Chart *What is Needed?/Practically and Theoretically*
(Was tut not?/Praktisch und Theoretisch)

Insert
Kinetogram of the beginning of *Zeitlupe (Slow Motion)* from *Grünen Clowns
(Green Clowns),* choreographed by Dussia Bereska

VOL. II, NO. 2, MAY 1929

Schlemmer, Oskar, Drawing on cover *Man-Machine* (Mensch-Maschine)
Snell, Gertrud, *Foundation for a General Theory of Dance, Part II Choreology* (Grundlagen einer allgemeinen Tanzlehre, II Choreologie)
Dressler, Ernst Christoph, *A Few Questions* (Einige Fragen) (1777)
Gregor, Joseph, *A Theory of the Pageant* (Theorie des Festzuges)
Klingenbeck, Fritz, *The Dancing Pageant* (Der tanzende Festzug)
Rudolph, Charlotte, *Dance Photography* (Tanzphotographie)

Discussion (Diskussion)
Götze, Will, *Dance Accompaniment* (Tanzbegleitung)
Gutheim, Karlheinz, *Dance with a Mechanical Piano* (Tanz mit mechanischem Klavier)
Wilckens, Friedrich, *Dance with a Mechanical Organ* (Tanz mit mechanischer Orgel)
Schlee, Alfred, *Closing Remarks* (Schlusswort)
Engelhardt, Gustav, *Notation According to Zorn* (Choreographie nach Zorn)
Proceedings of the German Association for Written Dance (Mitteilungen der deutschen Gesellschaft für Schrifttanz)

News Items (Notizen)
Janowitz, *Music for Dance* (a collected list, classified by rhythm) (Tanzbare Musik)

Insert
Kinetogram, *Preliminary Exercises for a Dance* (Vorübungen zu einem Tanz)

VOL. II, NO. 3, AUGUST 1929

Heckroth, Heinrich, *Costume Design* on cover
Landes, H., *Dance* (Tanz)
Urbach, Franz, *Freeing the Rhythm* (Befreiung des Rhythmus)
Snell, Gertrud, *Foundations for a General Theory of Dance, Part III Eukinetics* (Grundlagen einer allgemeinen Tanzlehre, III Eukinetik)
Hoffmann, Willy, *The Protection of Copyright in the Art of Dance* (Der Urheberrechtsschutz der Tanzkunst)
Burian, E.F., *Dance with Words* (Worttanz)
Wang, Cilli, *Dance Based on the Spoken Word* (Der Tanz nach gesprochenem Wort)

Reviews (Umschau)
Knab, Armin, *Mary Wigman 'Visionen'* (Visions)
Dr. B., *Rudolf von Laban 'Alltag und Fest'* (Everyday and Festival)
Lewitan, Joseph, *The Diaghilev Ballet* (Das Diaghileff-Ballett)

Book and Music Reviews (Bücher und Noten)
Rohlsen, Helmuth, *Das Werk Fritz Böhmes* (The Work of Fritz Böhme)
Neue tänzerische Musik in der Universal Edition (New Music for Dance from Universal Edition)
Atlantis monthly journal, Verlag Wasmuth

Proceedings of the German Association for Written Dance (Mitteilungen der deutschen Gesellschaft für Schrifttanz)

News Items (Notizen)
Season's programme from the theatres (vom Spielplan der Theater)

Insert
Kinetogram of part of Laban's *Alltag und Fest*

VOL. II, NO. 4, DECEMBER 1929

Heckroth, Heinrich, *Line Drawing of Rudolf von Laban* on cover
Wigman, Mary, *Rudolf von Laban for his Birthday* (Rudolf von Laban zum Geburtstag)
Böhme, Fritz, *Laban's new Generation of Dancers* (Labans tänzerischer Nachwuchs)·
Gleisner, Martin, *Laban as Creator of Amateur Dance and the Movement Choir* (Laban als Schöpfer von Laientanz und Bewegungschor)
Brandenburg, Hans, *Memories of Laban's Beginnings* (Erinnerungen an Labans Anfänge)
Wulff, Käthe, *From Old Letters* (Aus alten Briefe); *Data from Laban's Life and Work* (Daten aus Labans Leben und Wirken)

Discussion (Diskussion)
Klingenbeck, Fritz, *Writing and Reading* [with notation examples] (Schreiben und Lesen)

Plates
Laban, Rudolf von, *Movement Study in Oil, 1898* (Bewegungsstudie in Öl, 1898)
Laban, Rudolf von, *Self Portrait, 1902* (Selbstportrait, 1902)
Heckroth, Heinrich, *Rudolf von Laban, 1929*
Robertson, (photo) *Rudolf von Laban's hands, 1929* (Die Hände Rudolf von Labans, 1929)

Book Reviews (Buchbesprechung)
Victor Junk, *Handbuch des Tanzes* (Dance Handbook), Ernst-Klett Verlag
Karl Vogt, *Praxis des Sprechchores* (Speech Choir Practice), Verlag Der Sturm

Proceedings of the German Association for Written Dance (Mitteilungen der deutschen Gesellschaft für Schrifttanz)

News Items (Notizen)
Request for readers to publicise *Schrifttanz* (An unsere Leser!)

VOL. III, NO. 1, APRIL 1930

Monteiras, de Rego, *Movement Study of Anna Pavlova* on cover
Schlee, Alfred, *At the Turning Point of the New Dance* (An der Wende des neuen Tanzes)
Nijinska, Bronislava, *On Movement and the School of Movement* (Von der Bewegung und der Schule der Bewegung)
Thomas, Irmgard, *Ballet as Educator* (Ballett als Erzieher)
Gautier, Theophile, *A Saying* (Ein Ausspruch) (1850)
Sandt, Alfred, *Dance in Opera of the 18th Century* (Der Tanz in der Oper des 18. Jahrhunderts)
Jodjana, Raden A., *On Javanese Dance* (Vom javanischen Tanz)

Review (Umschau)
Brandenburg, Hans, *'Totenmal' (Memorial) and Dance* (*Totenmal* und Tanz)
Third Dancers' Congress: announcement

Discussion
Neumann, Konrad, *Dance Notation* (Tanzschrift)
Gleisner, Martin, *Reply* (Entgegnung)
Proceedings of the German Association for Written Dance (Mitteilungen der deutschen Gesellschaft für Schrifttanz)

News Items (Notizen)

Insert
Kinetogram of *Ballet Exercise at the Barre*

VOL. III, NO. 2, JUNE 1930

Kirsta, Georg, *Costume Sketch for a Dance for the Kammertanzbühne Bereska* on cover
Klingenbeck, Fritz, *Technique and Form* (Technik und Form)
Güldenstein, Gustav, *Foundations for a Dance Culture* (Grundlagen zu einer Tanzkultur)
Laban, Rudolf von, *On the Nature of the Movement Choir* (Vom Sinn der Bewegungschöre)
Müller-Rau, Elli, *'Kitsch'*

Martin, John, *Modern Dance in America* (Der moderne Tanz in Amerika)
Clouzot, Marie-Rose, *Modern Ballet Décor in France* (Moderne Ballett-Dekorationen in Frankreich)
Moroda, Derra de, *Enrico Cecchetti*
Wellesz, Egon, *The 'Balletto a cavallo'*

Plates
Balletto a cavallo
Picasso, *Figurine*
Chirico, *Le Bal*
Lagut, Irene, *Les mariés de la Tour Eiffel*
Larionoff, *Quatre saisons*
(photo) *Cecchetti with Serge Lifar*

Reviews (Umschau)
Böhme, Fritz, *Imagination and Experience in Dance/'Gaukelei' (Jugglery)*, *'Drosselbart'*, *'Schwingende Landschaft' (Swinging Landscape)* (Vorstellung und Erlebnis im Tanz)
Felber, Erwin, *Stage Festival in Delphi* (Bühnenfestspiele in Delphi)
Schlee, Alfred, *Dancers' Congress – Memories* (Tänzerkongress – Erinnerung)

Book and Music Reviews (Bücher und Noten)
Monographien der Ausbildungsschulen für Tanz und tänzerische Körperbildung Vol. 1 (Monographs on the Training Schools for Dance and Exercises for Dance), Liesel Freund (ed.), Leo Alterthum-Verlag
Hansjürgen Wille, *Harald Kreutzberg – Yvonne Georgi*, Verlag Erich Weibzahl
Fernand Divoire, *Découvertes sur la Danse* (Discoveries about Dance), G. Cres et Cie
André Levinson, *La Danse d'aujourd'hui* (Dance of Today), Duchartre et Van Buggenhoudt
Joachim Stutschewsky, *Vier Jüdische Tanzstücke* (Four Jewish Dance Pieces), Universal Edition

Proceedings of the German Association for Written Dance (Mitteilungen der deutschen Gesellschaft für Schrifttanz)

News Items (Notizen)

Insert
Kinetogram from a 'Festlicher Marsch' (Festive March) by Albrecht Knust

VOL. III, NO. 3, NOVEMBER 1930

Hiler, *Untitled Line Drawing* on cover
Günther, Dorothée, *Why Dance Pedagogy?* (Warum Tanzpädagogik?)
Anon., *The Material of Ballet Action* (Vom Stoff der Balletthandlung)
Klingenbeck, Fritz, *What Should one Write down and What not?* (Was aufschreiben und was nicht?)
Kirsta, Georg, *Concerning Dance Costume* (Vom Tanzkostüm)
Skoronel, Vera, *Mary Wigman's Style of Composition/Comments on 'Swinging Landscape'* (Mary Wigmans Kompositionsstil/Bemerkungen zur 'Schwingende Landschaft')
Divoire, Fernand, *Dance in Paris* (Der Tanz in Paris)
Rumness, Alexander, *Dance in Soviet Russia* (Tanz in Sowjetrußland)
Schlee, Alfred, *Dancers' Congress in Munich* (Tänzerkongress in München)

Reviews (Umschau)
Zoltán Kodály, *Marosszéker Tänze,* Universal Edition
George Antheil, *Tango aus der Oper 'Transatlantic',* Universal Edition
Tänzerische Musik (Music for Dance), joint publication by Russian State Press and Universal Edition
Isadora Duncan, *The Art of the Dance,* New York Theatre Arts, *Theatre Arts Monthly* (New York)
The Artists of the Dance, British Continental Press

Proceedings of the German Association for Written Dance (Mitteilungen der deutschen Gesellschaft für Schrifttanz)

New Items (Notizen)

VOL. IV, NO. 1, JUNE 1931

Larionoff, M., *Costume Design for Clothilde von Derp-Saccharoff* on cover
Kállai, Ernst, *Between Ritual and Cabaret* (Zwischen Kulttanz und Varieté)
Gert, Valeska, *Dancing* (Tanzen)
Laban, Rudolf von, *Anna Pavlova*
Jencik, Joe, *Kokain: an Attempt at an Analysis of Anita Berber's Dance* (Kokain: Versuch einer Analyse des Tanzes von Anita Berber)
Böhme, Fritz, *About Contre-Tanz and Notation* (Über Contre und Contre-Choreographie)
Loesch, Ilse, *Education in Written Dance* (Ausbildung zum Schrifttanz)
Knust, Albrecht, *Contributions to the Orthography of Movements* (Beiträge zur Orthographie von Bewegungen)
Brasch, *On Dance Criticism* (Über die Tanzkritik)
Schlee, Alfred, *Olimpiade della grazia in Florence*

Plates

Abbé, (photo) *Anna Pavlova*

Contretanz – Choreographie (Notation of Contre-Tanz)

Larionoff, M., *Costume Design for Clothilde von Derp-Saccharoff*

Anon., (photo) *Anita Berber and Droste*

New Books

Terpsichora, Jan Reimoser Verlag

Valeska Gert, *Mein Weg* (My Way), F.A. Devrient

Klingenbeck, Fritz, *Dance notation in plays* (Tanzschrift im Schauspiel)

News Items and Proceedings of the German Association for Written Dance
   (Notizen und Mitteilungen der deutschen Gesellschaft für Schrifttanz)
The Ballet Club
Work in the Theatre
Summer Courses
Miscellaneous

VOL. IV, NO. 2, OCTOBER 1931

Schlemmer, Oskar, *Drawing* on cover

Schlemmer, Oskar, *Misunderstandings* (Mißverständnisse)

Knust, Albrecht, *The Kinetogram Publications of the Hamburg Dance Notation Bureau* (Die Kinetogramm-Veröffentlichungen der Hamburger Tanzschreibstube)

Hasting, Hanns, *Sound and Space* (Klang und Raum)

Redlich, Hans F., *The Function of Music in the Günther-Schule* (Die Funktion der Musik im Rahmen der Günther-Schule)

Günther, Dorothée, *Die Barbarische Suite (Barbaric Suite)*

Gleisner, Martin, *Festival Work 'Rotes Lied' (Red Song)*

Jemnitz, Alexander, *Dance, Sonata, and Dance-sonata* (Tanz, Sonate und Tanzsonate)

Divoire, Fernand, *From Paris* (Aus Paris)

News items and Proceedings of the German Association for Written Dance
   (Notizen und Mitteilungen der deutschen Gesellschaft für Schrifttanz)

Insert

Kinetogram of *Exercises* by Albrecht Knust

Main Periodicals which Carried Articles on Dance

Dance and Dance-Related

Der Bewegungschor, 1928
Edited Paul Weichelt, monthly illustrated magazine of the Society for the Promotion of Movement Choirs, published in Hamburg.

Gymnastik und Tanz, 1926–43
Edited Franz Hilker, magazine for physical education and dance, published in Dresden and from 1935 in Berlin.

Illustrierte Tanz-Zeitung, 1921–22
Edited Gudrun Hildebrandt, published in Berlin–Charlottenburg.

Körperrhythmus und Tanz, 1929
Edited G.Jo. Vischer-Klamt, newsletter of the Jutta-Klamt Society (association of pupils, friends and founders of the Jutta-Klamt School), published in Berlin.

Das Podium, 1920–35
Half-monthly magazine for the performing arts, published in Berlin.

Der Rhythmus, 1922–43
Edited Dr Hans Frucht and Dr Rudolf Bode, newsletter of the Bode Association, published in Munich, Kassel (1930–34) and Berlin (1934–43).

Singchor und Tanz, 1928–35
Edited Carl Schönherr, half-monthly journal for professional singers and dancers, published in Mannheim.

Der Tanz, 1919–21
Edited Ludwig Hann, half-monthly magazine for theatrical and social dance, published in Vienna.

Der Tanz, 1927–43
Edited Joseph Lewitan, monthly magazine for theatrical and social dance, published in Berlin (except 1927, Munich, and 1931, Leipzig).

Die Tanzgemeinschaft, 1929–30
Edited G.Jo. Vischer-Klamt and Dr Felix Emmel, quarterly journal of dance and rhythmic gymnastics, published in Berlin.

Terpsichore, 1923
Edited Albert Nicolaus and Jürgen Schmidt, official publication of the General German Dance Teachers Association, published in Berlin.

General

Die Aktion, 1911–32
Edited Franz Pfembert, weekly magazine for liberal politics, literature and art, published in Berlin.

Die Freude, 1924–29
Edited Robert Laurer, monthly naturist magazine, published in Hamburg.

Jugend, 1896–1940
Edited Georg Hirth, monthly satirical illustrated magazine on Munich's artistic and cultural life.

Die Jugendbühne, 1920–32
Magazine for young people's theatre, published in Osterwieck.

Die Kontakt, 1933
Edited G.Jo. Vischer-Klamt, quarterly magazine of physical education, published in Berlin.

Die Musik, 1901–43
Edited Arthur Seidl (1901–10) and Bernhard Schuster, monthly musical journal, published first in Leipzig and Berlin, and from 1922 in Stuttgart.

Die neue Schaubühne, 1919–25
Edited Hugo Zehder and Heinar Schilling, monthly magazine of stage, theatre and screen, published first in Berlin, and from 1920 in Dresden.

Der Querschnitt, 1921–36
Edited Hermann von Wedderkorp, magazine for contemporary culture, published in Berlin.

Der Scheinwerfer, 1927–33
Edited Hannes Küpper, newsletter of the city theatre in Essen, and published there.

Die Schönheit, 1906–26
Edited Richard A. Giesecke, half-yearly illustrated naturist magazine, published in Dresden.

Simplicissimus, 1896–1944
Founding editors Albert Langer and T.Th. Heine, weekly illustrated satirical magazine, published in Munich.

Der Sturm, 1910–32
Edited Herwath Walden, weekly, half-monthly from 1913, monthly from 1920, magazine of Expressionism in culture and the arts, published in Berlin.

Die Szene, 1910–33
Edited Ferdinand Gregori, monthly magazine for the theatre, published in Berlin–Charlottenburg.

Die Tat, 1909–39
Edited Dr Eugen Diederichs, monthly magazine for the promotion of new ideas in culture, published in Jena.
Der Vortrupp, 1912–21
Edited R. Kraut and Hermann L. Poperl, half-monthly magazine for the promotion of German culture, published first in Leipzig, and from 1914 in Hamburg.

Biographical Notes on Contributors to the Articles Included in these Translations

Fritz Böhme (1881–1952) Leading dance historian and critic during the 1920s and 1930s.

Alfred Brasch Author of several articles on the relationship between theatre and dance.

Lasar Galpern Ballet-master in Düsseldorf and Cologne.

Valeska Gert (1892–1978) Famous Berlin recital performer of the 1920s who combined dance with theatre, mime and cabaret. Her performances were satirical and socially critical. When the Nazis came to power she emigrated to the USA and made her living as a film actress, returning to Germany after the war.

Martin Gleisner (1897–1983) Leader of Laban's movement choirs in Berlin and Gera. Author of several choral and educational works including *Tanz für Alle* (1928). In 1933 he became a refugee, eventually settling in the USA in 1940.

Gustav Güldenstein Involved in the educational dance movement. Writer of several articles on the significance of artistic dance and rhythmic exercise in education during the early 1930s.

Dorothée Günther (1896–1975) German teacher of dance and rhythmic exercise. Pupil of Dalcroze and Laban. Worked with composer Carl Orff at her Munich school. In 1933 she founded a dance group and a school in Berlin together with Berthe Trümpy. In 1945 she emigrated to Rome.

Hanns Hasting Musical director of the Wigman School and a composer for the dance. Contributed articles on the relationship of dance and music to *Die Musik*.

Joe Jancik Choreographer at the Czech National Theatre in 1937.

Ernst Kállai Dance critic for the *Sozialistische Monatshefte* from 1930 to 1933 to which he contributed regular features on dance and dancers. In the late 1920s he also wrote occasionally for *Der Sturm*.

Georg Kirsta Stage and costume designer for ballet. Collaborated with Lizzie Maudrik in Berlin and Yvonne Georgi in Hanover. Occasional writer on ballet and choreography.

Fritz Klingenbeck (b. 1904) Austrian dancer, writer and theatre director. Student of Laban in 1928 and then his assistant; soloist and ballet-master in Berlin, Prague and Vienna.

Armin Knab (1881–1951) Composer.

Albrecht Knust (1896–1978) Teacher and choreographer. An early student of Laban's who was a member of Laban's Tanzbühne. His main achievement was in promotion of Laban's notation, of which he became the international authority, writing *Dictionary of Kinetography Laban* in 1951.

Rudolf von Laban (1879–1958) Leading dance reformer, contributed to dance theatre, community dance, dance education, and dance literacy in Germany. From 1938 in the UK where he started dance therapy, dance for children, and was actively involved in movement for actors and work study in industry. With Lisa Ullmann started the Art of Movement Studio, Manchester (1946) which is now the Laban Centre for Movement and Dance in London.

Joseph Lewitan Editor of *Der Tanz* and dance critic in Berlin.

Lizzie Maudrik (1898–1955) Danced in Laban's *Don Juan*. Ballet-mistress of the Berlin Städtische Oper, and in 1934 of the Staatsoper.

Bronislava Nijinska (1891–1972) Danced in the Diaghilev Ballet along with her brother Vaslav. Returned to Russia in 1914 to open her School of Movement in Kiev. Worked for Diaghilev and independently as a choreographer. Principal works *Les Noces* and *Les Biches*.

Hans Redlich (1903–68) Born in Vienna where he began his early music education which led to a successful musical career as conductor in Berlin and Mainz in the early 1920s. Emigrated to Britain in 1939 for political reasons and acquired citizenship in 1947. He was a renowned musicologist, author, editor and lecturer.

Charlotte Rudolph Dance photographer.

Alfred Schlee (b. 1904) Editor of *Schrifttanz,* music publisher with Universal Edition, Vienna, promoter of new music, opera and dance, and of dance notation.

Oskar Schlemmer (1888–1943) German painter, sculptor and choreographer. Headed the Stage Workshop at the Bauhaus from 1923 to 1928. His innovations in dance costume and spatial design are exemplified in his well-known works *Triadic Ballet* and *The Bauhaus Dances.*

Irmgard Thomas School for ballet in Vienna. Involved in the educational dance movement.

Berthe Trümpy (1895–1983) Swiss dancer, pupil and later assistant of Mary Wigman. In 1926 she directed her own school with Vera Skoronel in Berlin.

Mary Wigman (1886–1973) Leading dancer and choreographer. Started with Dalcroze. Worked with Laban in Munich and Ascona, toured solo programme in Switzerland and Germany. Founded her school in Dresden. Three American tours between 1930 and 1933.

Notes on Photographs

Figure 1.   Oskar Schlemmer: *Triadic Ballet,* 1926
photo: anon.
in Schlemmer, Oskar, *The Letters and Diaries of Oskar
Schlemmer* (ed. Tut Schlemmer, tr. Winston Krisham), Middletown, Conn.: Wesleyan Univ. Press, 1975

Figure 2.   Oskar Schlemmer: *Pole Dance,* 1927
photo: anon.
in Schlemmer, Oskar, *The Letters and Diaries of Oskar
Schlemmer* (ed. Tut Schlemmer, tr. Winston Krisham), Middletown, Conn.: Wesleyan Univ. Press, 1975

Figure 3.   Valeska Gert, 1930
photo: anon.
in *Tänzerinnennder Gegenwart,* Zürich: Füssli Verlag, 1931

Figure 4.   Choreographisches Institut Laban, 1928
photo: Keystone View Company, Berlin
in Freund, Liesel (ed.), *Monographien der Ausbildungsschulen
für Tanz und tänzerische Körperbildung,* Berlin: Alterthum
Verlag, 1929

Figure 5.   Choreographisches Institut Laban: Laban and class, clowning,
1927 *(from l. to r.:* Dussia Bereska, Gertrud Snell, Ilse Loesch,
Beatrice Loeb, Martin Gleisner, Rudolf von Laban, Gert Ruth
Loeszer)
photo: anon., Laban Collection

Figure 6.   Hamburg Movement Choir Men's Group: *Canon in Space,* 1926
(leader Albrecht Knust)
photo: anon., Laban Collection

Figure 7.   Hertha Feist's Laban School: *Men's Dance,* 1925
photo: anon., Laban Collection

Figure 8.   Jenny Gertz's Children's Movement Choir, 1926
photo: anon., Laban Collection

Figures 9,   Amateur dancers from Hertha Feist's Laban School in the Berlin
10 and 11.   Stadium, 1923
photos: anon., Laban Collection

Figure 12.   Mary Wigman with students in *Dreieck (Triangle),* 1930
photo: anon.
in *Sie und Er,* No. 49, 1931

Figure 13.   Mary Wigman, 1930
photo: Charlotte Rudolph, Dresden
in Aubel, Hermann and Marianne, *Der künstlerische Tanz
unserer Zeit,* Leipzig: Blaue Bücher, 1930

Figure 14.   Essen Dancers' Congress, 1928 (*front row, l. to r.*: Olga Brandt-
Knack, Heinrich Kröller, Max Terpis, Lizzie Maudrik, Gertrud
Snell, Hans Brandenburg, Berthe Trümpy, Rudolf von Laban,
Dussia Bereska, Alfred Schlee, Vera Skoronel, Fritz Böhme,
Manda von Kreibig; *back row, l. to r.*: Harald Fürstenau, Aurel
von Milloss, ?, Hertha Feist, Sigurd Leeder, Hanns Niedecken-
Gebhardt, Kurt Jooss, ?, ?)
photo: Robertson, Berlin

Figure 15.   *Anita Berber* by Otto Dix, 1925
photo: anon.
in Fischer, Lothar, *Anita Berber/Tanz zwischen Rausch und
Tod,* Berlin: Haude & Spenersche Verlagsbuchhandlung, 1984

Figure 16.   Vera Skoronel's Dance Group
photo: Suse Byk, Berlin

Figure 17.   Tanzbühne Laban in his dance tragedy *Gaukelei,* 1923
photo: K. Schellenberg
in *Die Schönheit,* 1926

Figure 18.   Rudolf von Laban and Gert Ruth Loeszer, 1925
photo: anon., from F. Klingenbeck

Figure 19. Rudolf von Laban and Berlin State Opera dancers, 1930
photo: anon., from Martin Gleisner Collection

Figure 20. Harald Kreutzberg and Yvonne Georgi in *Stravinsky Suite,* 1928
photo: Robertson, Berlin
in Fischer, Hans W., *Körper, Schönheit und Körperkultur,*
Berlin: Deutsche Buchgemeinschaft, 1928

Figure 21. Max Terpis: *Der Letzte Pierrot (The Last Pierrot),* 1929
photo: Robertson, Berlin
in Freund, Liesel (ed.), *Monographien der Ausbildungsschulen
für Tanz und tänzerische Körperbildung,* Berlin: Alterthum
Verlag, 1929

Bibliography

The books listed below form only part of the authors' resources. Additional material used comes from the Laban Collection and consists of personal letters, programmes, newspaper cuttings, interviews and photographs.

A list of magazines of the period either specialising in dance or containing regular features on dance is given in Appendix II.

The bibliography is selective, especially in areas which are well documented – such as the Diaghilev period, the Bauhaus and Expressionism. Included are primary sources from the period as well as a selection of recent publications in English.

German Sources

BACH, Rudolf, *Das Mary Wigman Werk*. Dresden: Carl Reissner Verlag, 1933

BLASS, Ernst, *Das Wesen der neuen Tanzkunst*. Weimar: Erich Lichtenstein Verlag, 1922

BOLLIGER, Hans; Magnaguagno, Guido; Meyer, Raimond, *Dada in Zürich*. Zürich: Kunsthaus Zürich und Arche Verlag, 1985

BRANDENBURG, Hans, *Der moderne Tanz*. München: Georg Müller, 1921 (2nd extended edn)

FISCHER, Hans W., *Das Tanzbuch*. München, Albert Langen, 1924
Körper, Schönheit und Körperkultur. Berlin: Deutsche Buchgemeinschaft, GmbH, 1928

FISCHER, Lothar, *Anita Berber/Tanz zwischen Rausch und Tod*. Berlin: Haude & Spenersche Verlagsbuchhandlung, 1984

GIESE, Frank, *Körperseele*. München, Delphin Verlag, 1924

JESCHKE, Claudia, *Tanzschriften: Ihre Geschichte und Methode*. Bad Reichenhall: Comes Verlag, 1983

LABAN, Rudolf von, *Die Welt des Tänzers*. Stuttgart: Chr. Belserschen Buchdruckerei, 1920
Choreographie. Jena: Eugen Diederichs Verlag, 1926
Des Kindes Gymnastik und Tanz. Oldenburg: Gerhardt Stalling Verlag, 1926

Schrifttanz: Methodik, Orthographie, Erläuterungen. Wien: Universal Edition, 1928

Gymnastik und Tanz. Oldenburg: Gerhardt Stalling Verlag, 1929

Ein Leben für den Tanz. Dresden: Carl Reissner Verlag, 1935

MAACK, Rudolf, *Tanz in Hamburg.* Hamburg: Hans Christians Verlag, 1975

MENSENDIECK, Bess, *Körperkultur der Frau.* München: F. Bruckmann, 1925

MUELLER, Hedwig, *Mary Wigman, Leben und Werk der grossen Tänzerin.* Weinheim: Quadriga, 1986

PETER, Frank Manuel, *Valeska Gert.* Berlin: Verlag Fröhlich und Kaufmann, 1985

SCHIKOWSKI, John, *Der neue Tanz.* Berlin, 1924

Geschichte des Tanzes. Berlin: Büchergilde Gutenberg, 1926

SCHUFTAN, Werner, *Handbuch des Tanzes.* Mannheim: Verlag Deutscher Chorsänger Verband und Tänzerbund EV, 1928

SCHUR, Ernst, *Der moderne Tanz.* München: Gustav Lammers, 1910

STEINBECK, Dietrich, *Mary Wigmans choreographisches Skizzenbuch 1930–1961.* Berlin: Akademie der Künste, Berlin; Edition Hentrich Berlin, 1987

SUHR, Werner, *Der künstlerische Tanz.* Leipzig: Linnemann, 1920

SZEEMANN, Harald (ed.), *Monte Verità.* Milan: Electra Editrice, 1978

Der Hang zum Gesamtkunstwerk. Aarau: Verlag Sauerländer, 1983

TANZ 20. JAHRHUNDERT IN WIEN/Ausstellungskatalog. Wien: Österreichisches Theatermuseum, 1979

THIESS, Frank, *Der Tanz als Kunstwerk.* München, Delphin Verlag, 1920

WIGMAN, Mary, *Deutsche Tanzkunst.* Dresden: Carl Reissner Verlag, 1935

WINTHER, Fritz, *Körperbildung als Kunst und Pflicht.* München, Delphin Verlag, 1915

English Sources

BUCKLE, Richard, *Diaghilev.* London: Weidenfeld & Nicolson, 1979

CARDINAL, Roger, *Expressionism.* London: Paladin Books, 1984

COTON, A.V., *The New Ballet/Kurt Jooss and his Work.* London: Dennis Dobson, 1946

DALCROZE, Emile Jaques, *Rhythm, Music and Education.* London: Riverside Press, first pub. 1921, new edn 1967

GREEN, Martin, *Mountain of Truth/The Counter Culture Begins, Ascona 1900–1920.* Hanover and London: pub. for Tufts Univ. by Univ. Press of New England, 1986

GROPIUS, Walter (ed.), *The Theatre of the Bauhaus.* Middletown, Conn.: Wesleyan Univ. Press, 1961

HASKELL, Arnold, *Diaghileff, His Artistic and Private Life.* London: Victor Gollancz, 1935

HUTCHINSON GUEST, Ann, *Dance Notation, the Process of Recording on Paper*. London: Dance Books, 1987

JORDAN, Diana, *The Dance as Education*. London: Oxford Univ. Press, 1938

KANDINSKY, Wassily, *Concerning the Spiritual in Art*. New York: Dover Publications, 1977

KNUST, Albrecht, *A Dictionary of Kinetography Laban (Labanotation)*, Vols. 1 & 2. Plymouth: Macdonald & Evans, 1979

LABAN, Rudolf von, *Modern Educational Dance*. London: Macdonald & Evans, 1948

Principles of Dance and Movement Notation. London: Macdonald & Evans, 1956

A Life for Dance (tr. Lisa Ullmann). London: Macdonald & Evans, 1975

MALETIC, Vera, *Body–Space–Expression*. Berlin: Mouton de Gruyter, 1987

MARKARD, Anna & Hermann, *Jooss*. Köln: Ballett-Bühnen-Verlag, 1985

MONEY, Keith, *Anna Pavlova, Her Life and Art*. London: Collins, 1982

PATTERSON, Michael, *The Revolution in German Theatre*. London: Routledge & Kegan Paul, 1981

SCHLEMMER, Oskar, *The Letters and Diaries of Oskar Schlemmer* (ed. Tut Schlemmer, tr. Winston Krisham). Middletown, Conn.: Wesleyan Univ. Press, 1972

SORELL, Walter, *The Mary Wigman Book*. Middletown, Conn.: Wesleyan Univ. Press, 1975

Dance in its Time. Garden City, NY: Anchor Press, 1981

WIGMAN, Mary, *The Language of Dance*. London: Macdonald & Evans, 1966

WILLET, John, *The New Sobriety 1917–1933/Art and Politics in the Weimar Period*. London: Thames & Hudson, 1978

Index of Names